T0018875

Does

the

Bible

Affirm

Same-Sex

Relationships?

Examining 10 Claims about
Scripture and Sexuality

Rebecca McLaughlin

"This is a timely and sensitive book that offers a positive vision for human relationships. It shows that responsible handling of the Bible can lead to more love, not less."

Peter Williams, Principal, Tyndale House;
Author, *Can We Trust the Gospels?*

"With sensitivity, faithfulness, and clarity, Rebecca McLaughlin addresses ten questions often raised about the Bible and same-sex relationships. For each, she deftly engages with different interpretations of the Bible's teaching and, in dialogue with personal stories, provides a more compelling interpretation. A most helpful book for anyone wanting concise, accessible, sensitive, and biblically faithful approaches to these questions."

James Robson, Principal,
Oak Hill Theological College, London

"Rebecca McLaughlin is not afraid to tackle the toughest questions our culture has for Christianity, and in this short book she has again shown her willingness to teach biblical truth clearly, straightforwardly, and compassionately. I hope this book is widely read by both those who agree and those who disagree."

Kathy Keller, Author, *Jesus, Justice, and Gender Roles*

"With characteristic clarity and compassion, Rebecca McLaughlin examines the most common arguments that Christians use to support the idea that God affirms same-sex relationships. Careful and nuanced argument will help the reader have confidence in what the Bible does teach—and assurance that it is good news for everyone, including those who experience same-sex attraction."

Ros Clarke, Associate Director, Church Society

"This is outstanding: short, readable, warm, well illustrated, clear, and gracious. Rebecca's blend of personal experience, biblical study, and cultural wisdom is richly displayed in this book, and it is just what we need."

Andrew Wilson, Teaching Pastor, King's Church London

"It can be easy for Christians today to wonder if we've got it wrong on an issue as high-stakes as same-sex sexuality. Deeply biblical, and illustrated in real-life examples, Rebecca McLaughlin's book shows us the Bible's consistent and compelling vision for human sexuality. Christians will find this illuminating, reassuring, and deeply encouraging."

Sam Allberry, Associate Pastor, Immanuel Nashville; Author, *Is God Anti-gay?*

"This book explains in a powerful, clear, and compelling way what the Bible says about same-sex relationships. I love Rebecca's writing. She writes with humility, precision, and faithfulness, and the gospel testimony that comes through it is beautiful. You'll come away from this book not only better informed but more in awe of God's incredible, sustaining grace."

J.D. Greear, Pastor, The Summit Church, Raleigh-Durham, NC; Council Member, The Gospel Coalition

"This book offers gentle correction to those who long for a biblical reinterpretation that allows for same-sex marriage, while also offering a liberating vision of singleness and relationship intimacy within the body of Christ. McLaughlin shows how a truly biblical understanding of sexuality focuses all of us on Jesus. This is an important and grace-filled little book."

Darryl Williamson, Lead Pastor, Living Faith Bible Fellowship, Tampa, FL

For Paige,
my beloved sister

Does the Bible Affirm Same-Sex Relationships?
© Rebecca McLaughlin, 2024

Published by
The Good Book Company

thegoodbook.com | thegoodbook.co.uk
thegoodbook.com.au | thegoodbook.co.nz | thegoodbook.co.in

Design by Faceout Studio / The Good Book Company

ISBN: 9781784989712 | JOB-007660 | Printed in India

Contents

Introduction:
A Tale of
Two Testimonies

When I showed up at Cambridge for my undergrad degree, I had a secret. I'd been a follower of Jesus for as long as I could remember. But as soon as I was old enough to have romantic feelings, they'd homed in on other girls. I'd hoped it was just a phase. After all, I was in single-sex education. Maybe I just hadn't met enough guys. I told myself that when I went to university, I'd start to fall for men. But my feet had barely touched the ground at Cambridge when I started having feelings for a female friend.

I felt embarrassed. I'd told a handful of people over the years, but it was extremely hard to talk about. I wanted to get married one day, but I was a passionate Christian, and I was convinced that the Bible was against same-sex relationships, so I felt stuck. I tried to wait out my feelings, still swearing to myself that it was just a phase. But by the time I started my Ph.D., I could no longer swallow my own story. My tendency to fall in love with women wasn't an adolescent phase. It felt more like a waste: a secret, pointless, painful sadness that I could not shake.

Meanwhile, thousands of miles away, my (now) friend Rachel was starting as an undergrad at Yale. She'd grown up in a non-religious home in California, and she felt sure that there was no God. Aged fifteen, while studying with a female friend, Rachel had been struck by quite how beautiful her study partner was. This was no mere observation. It was a powerful attraction. So she started strategizing about how to turn this friendship sexual. Over time, they grew close, and when this friend asked Rachel what she wanted for her sixteenth birthday, Rachel replied that she wanted a kiss. This was the start of an on-and-off romance which lasted several years.

In the off times, Rachel pursued other pretty girls—some of whom identified as Christian. The fact that she could not only out-argue Christians but also seduce them added to her comfort in her atheism. But by the time she set off for college, Rachel was back with her first girlfriend, and she could not have been happier. Until her girlfriend broke up with her.

Rachel was devastated. She was already finding college hard. She'd excelled in high school, but she was struggling to keep up at Yale. So the blow to her heart of losing her girlfriend landed on top of a blow to her pride. "I wasn't thinking, *I should turn to Jesus*," Rachel recalls, "because I didn't believe in Jesus." But in her misery, a philosophy lecture made her wonder if she'd been too quick to rule out God. Rachel still felt confidently atheist, but she prided herself on knowledge. So she started googling religious terms. Without intending to, Rachel kept stumbling on stories about Jesus from the Bible.

The Jesus of the Bible was utterly unlike the Jesus Rachel had imagined. She'd thought of Jesus as a boring old conservative. But she discovered that he was not only radically loving but also incredibly smart. Rachel felt drawn to Jesus. But she also sensed a problem. She hoped to fall in love again and marry a woman someday, but she'd picked up that Christians were against same-sex marriage. Then again, the only two self-identifying Christians she knew at Yale were two women who were dating each other. So she went to visit them to ask how they had worked things out.

These two young women welcomed Rachel warmly and explained that there had been a big mistake: the Bible, read correctly, *does* affirm monogamous same-sex relationships. They gave her a booklet which laid out their case. Rachel read it eagerly and felt a surge of hope. But then she started googling the Bible passages the booklet referenced. As far as she could see, what the Bible said and what the booklet said seemed utterly at odds. So Rachel threw the booklet out in disappointment, kicking herself for wondering if there was room for her in Christianity.

Rachel thought that she was done with Jesus. But not long afterwards, she spotted a book titled *Mere Christianity* on a friend's bookshelf.[1] Ashamed to acknowledge her interest, Rachel stole the book. A few days later, as she was reading it in the library between classes, it burst on Rachel that there was a God. For a moment, she felt nothing but fear. She knew that this God was breathtakingly holy and that she was thoroughly sinful. It wasn't only that she had slept around. Rachel also knew that she was cruel and selfish. She had lied for fun and stolen things—including the book in her hands! Rachel recognized instinctively that she was guilty before God. But at that moment, she also understood for the first time that Jesus had stepped in to take the punishment for all her sin. As she sat there in the Yale library, Rachel knew that stepping into life with Jesus meant closing the door on same-sex romance. Yet Jesus' offer of forgiveness and eternal life and love seemed too good to refuse. So she took it.[2]

Your Story

I don't know what your story is when it comes to sexuality and Jesus. I don't know what hurts you carry or what hopes you harbor in your heart. I don't know if this book was put into your hands by somebody who wants to change your mind or if you're reading it because you don't know what to think yourself. I don't know if, like me, you have a lifelong history of same-sex attraction or if you're looking at these questions from the sidelines, so to speak. But whatever the reason, I'm so glad you're here!

Like the booklet Rachel was given by her college friends, this book works through some of the most popular arguments in favor of affirming same-sex sexual relationships for Christians—but it comes to the opposite conclusion: that the Bible does not affirm such relationships. In fact, it warns us in the strongest terms against them.

I'm painfully aware that covering so many arguments in such a short book might feel inadequate. But my aim has been to take seriously the ten claims that this book addresses. As far as it is possible in a short space, I've attempted to articulate each argument carefully, explore why it might seem persuasive, and explain where I think it falls short.

The first chapter looks at the big story of the Bible and why the question of same-sex relationships is not a question we can set aside. The second explores Jesus' words on marriage and on sexual sin. Chapters 3 and 4 work through Old Testament texts that reference same-sex sexual relationships. Chapters 5 to 8 examine the three New Testament texts that speak directly to this issue, through the lens of common questions. Chapters 9 and 10 seek to offer a biblical vision both for faithful singleness and for same-sex relationships of love that are not sexual or romantic.

Given my own lifelong history of same-sex attraction, you might think my conclusion—that the Bible leaves no room for followers of Jesus to pursue same-sex sexual relationships—makes this short book a tragedy. You might even think this book is an attempt to foster hatefulness toward those who identify as gay, lesbian, bisexual, or queer. But it is not. Instead of urging anybody toward hatred (of themselves or others), I hope instead to point us all to Jesus' love. And with Jesus' death-defying, life-creating, neverending love at the center of the picture, I want to sketch a vision from the Bible of deep, joyful, Christ-exalting love between believers of the same sex: not a love that mimics marriage but a no less precious, different kind of love.

Whatever your story and however you might feel as you begin this book, my hope is that it will act like a compass to help you navigate the Bible for yourself on this vital topic. My prayer is that like me, like Rachel, and like many other friends I'll mention in this book, you'll ultimately find that Jesus is the path to life and love beyond your wildest dreams.

CLAIM 1:
Christians Should Just Focus On The Gospel of God's Love

I n the first book in the *Harry Potter* series, Harry discovers the magical Mirror of Erised. In it, he sees his parents, who died when he was one. "Mum?" he whispers. "Dad?"[3] But when he tries to show his best friend, Ron, what he has found, Ron sees something else entirely. Later, Harry's mentor, Professor Dumbledore, explains: the mirror "shows us nothing more or less than the deepest, most desperate desire of our hearts."[4]

I wonder what you'd see if you gazed into such a mirror.

For most of us, at least at some point in our life, what we most desperately desire is one particular relationship. Perhaps you're in love, and you want nothing more than for that person to reciprocate your feelings. Perhaps you long for marriage, and you desperately desire to meet the man or woman of your dreams. Or maybe you are married, but the honest truth is that you've started having feelings toward someone other than your spouse—and it's those feelings that the mirror would expose.

We all know the power of romantic love and sexual desire. We know the ache of longing when our desires go unfulfilled. Whatever our own patterns of attraction, we also likely know people whose feelings gravitate toward their own sex. Could the Bible really say that such desire is wrong?

Especially in view of the history of some Christians acting genuinely hatefully toward those who identify as gay, the claim that the Bible says a clear "No" to same-sex sexual relationships strikes many people in the West today as both offensive and unjust. In fact, it puts off some people from even considering the claims of Jesus. So it's understandable that Christians sometimes ask, "Can't we just label this as a second-order issue, set it to the side, and focus on the gospel?"

As we work through the questions in this book, we'll see that we must take with deathly seriousness the Bible's warnings about any sexual relationships outside of male-female marriage. These warnings are so serious that the question of whether the Bible allows for same-sex sexual relationships cannot be set aside as a secondary issue on which Christians can agree to disagree. But we'll also see that the Bible's boundaries around sex are not just arbitrary. They're charcoal lines around a living picture of the most amazing love relationship we've ever seen—a love story so beautiful that it's been being told since the creation of the world. We'll see that rather than being a distraction *from* the gospel, God's design for Christian marriage is a pointer *to* the gospel. But to understand this story, we must trace our finger through the Bible from its first book to its last. So let's begin!

Biblical Big Picture

Some years ago, a semiretired lawyer told me about a time when he was working for a vehicle manufacturer whose new car design had been copied by a rival company. At the beginning of the trial, the lawyer placed a scale model of the car in question on the judge's desk. Days later, he discovered that the judge had totally misunderstood. Instead of recognizing that the miniature was just a copy of the real thing, the judge had thought the trial was about a model car! Too often, we are prone to make a similar mistake when we consider marriage. We imagine it's the ultimate relationship. But according to the Bible, it's just a scale model.

Like my lawyer friend, the Bible starts by showing us the model. The first chapter of the Bible tells us that God made us humans "in his own image … male and female" (Genesis 1:27). In the second chapter, we see God creating an individual man from the dust of the earth and a woman from his side. When God brings this man and woman together, we discover that their union is a prototype for future marriages: "Therefore a man shall leave his father and his mother and hold fast to his wife," we read, "and they shall become one flesh" (2:24). This husband and wife were naked and unashamed (v 25). So far, so "very good" (1:31). But in the Bible's third chapter, this first marriage gets messed up. The man and woman break the one commandment God has given them. Immediately, they realize that they're naked, and they try to hide from God. As Genesis 3 unfolds, we see that their sin has ruined their relationship with God and with each other (v 1-21).

This ancient story makes surprisingly good sense of our experience today. It tells us that our capacity for sexual relationships is part of God's extremely good design, and indeed we know that sex can be exhilarating and can forge a deep connection, as two people experience physical oneness. But Genesis also shows that our rejection of God's rule has blighted every aspect of our lives, not least our sexuality—and, yes, we can all sense that there's something deeply broken here as well. While humans can experience the joy of sexual intimacy, we can also feel the crushing pain when things go wrong. The agony of unrequited love. The poison of betrayal. The devastating force of sexual violence and abuse.

As we read on in the Bible, we see instances of all these things, from loving, faithful marriage to the wrecking ball of sexual sin. But we also hear prophets like Isaiah, Jeremiah, Ezekiel, and Hosea using marriage as a cosmic metaphor. Time and again, they picture God as a loving, faithful husband and Israel (God's Old Testament people) as his all too often faithless wife. "Your Maker is your husband," declares Isaiah, "the LORD of hosts is his name" (Isaiah 54:5). God's love never fails. But his people are continually breaking faith with him and turning to false gods. "Surely, as a treacherous wife leaves her husband," God says through Jeremiah, "so have you been treacherous to me, O house of Israel" (Jeremiah 3:20). This marriage between God and his people is in crisis. But then Jesus comes.

The Bridegroom

When asked why his disciples do not fast, Jesus replies, "Can the wedding guests fast while the bridegroom is with them?" (Mark 2:19).[5] The response is surprising. Jesus never married in his life on earth. So how is he the bridegroom? This is one of many moments in the New Testament Gospels when Jesus steps into the role of the Creator God of the Old Testament. Jesus claims he is the rightful husband to God's people.

John the Baptist (who was sent by God to get his people ready for his Son) also pictures Jesus in this way. When John is told that people who once followed him have started following Jesus, he replies:

The one who has the bride is the bridegroom. The friend of the bridegroom, who stands and hears

> *him, rejoices greatly at the bridegroom's voice.*
> *Therefore this joy of mine is now complete.*
>
> *(John 3:29)*

John is just a groomsman, helping at the wedding. So he's delighted when Jesus comes and claims God's people, like a bridegroom claiming his bride.

In the Old Testament, God's everlasting love and faithfulness were central to the marriage metaphor. God made a covenant with Israel, binding them to himself with promises. He pursued, protected, and provided for his people. In the New Testament, we see a shocking turn of events, as Jesus the bridegroom comes with love to take on flesh and *die* to save his bride. Now God's people includes anyone who puts their faith in Jesus—that is, the church.

So, what does this cosmic metaphor of a marriage between God and his people have to do with earthly marriage for believers now?

Model Marriage

Like the model car resembling the real vehicle, the apostle Paul presents Christian marriage as a scale model of the marriage between Jesus and his church. "Husbands, love your wives," Paul writes, "as Christ loved the church and gave himself up for her" (Ephesians 5:25). This call is drastic. Jesus loved the church by dying on a Roman cross. His people all together are his bride. So Jesus' love for his people becomes the model for how Christian husbands are to love their wives. Paul continues:

> *He who loves his wife loves himself. For no one ever hated his own flesh, but nourishes and cherishes it, just as Christ does the church, because we are members of his body. "Therefore a man shall leave his father and mother and hold fast to his wife, and the two shall become one flesh." This mystery is profound, and I am saying that it refers to Christ and the church. (v 28-32)*

According to Paul, the "one flesh" union between a husband and wife in Genesis 2:24 was always meant to model the oneness we can have with Jesus. Right from the beginning, when God made humans male and female—when he created sex and sexual desire and instituted marriage—he was building a scale model so that we could get a sense of just how passionately Jesus loves his church and just how intimately we can be united with him.

We see this marriage metaphor returning in the Bible's last book. Revelation pictures Jesus as "the Lamb who was slain" and describes a deafening shout going up: "The marriage of the Lamb has come, and his Bride has made herself ready" (Revelation 5:12; 19:7). The bride is the New Jerusalem—a double picture of God's people—and this great wedding happens at the center of God's new creation (21:1-3; 22:17). So Jesus' marriage to his church brings heaven and earth back together, as all God's people are made one with him and with each other.

To sum up: Christian marriage is designed to help us to wrap our minds round Jesus' exclusive, sacrificial, neverending, flesh-uniting, life-creating love for us. Marriage, rightly understood, is not a distraction from the gospel—it's a declaration of it.

So What?

This metaphor of Jesus' marriage to his people has two huge implications for how Christians must relate to marriage. First, it means that sexual and romantic love is not the gem-encrusted goal of life. Too often, Christians talk as if getting married must be every Christian's top priority and have no real vision for a faithful single life. But when we act like marriage is the thing we cannot truly live without, we make it an idol (or fake god) and undermine the gospel. Marriage is designed to be extremely good. But it's not ultimate. It is a scale model, not the real thing.

Second, because marriage is a model of a greater thing, it's vital that we stick with God's design. Just as Jesus' love for his people is a love across deep difference, so Christian marriage is a love across the deepest physical difference between humans: the sex difference that is written into every cell of our bodies. Jesus is both like us (human) and not like us (God).

Likewise, man and woman are both fundamentally alike and deeply different. Our relationship with Jesus is not one involving two interchangeable partners but a relationship of oneness across difference. So, male-female difference in marriage is not incidental to the model. It is an essential feature. Strikingly, it's union across this difference that makes it possible for humans to join God in his creation of new humans.

So can't Christians just focus on the gospel? Yes. We must. The gospel message of Jesus' love is at the heart of any truly Christian vision of sexuality. But just as everything that my lawyer friend was trying to argue made more sense when the judge realized that the case was not about model cars, so when we train our eyes on Jesus' love for his people, we'll find that what the Bible says on sexuality and marriage makes a whole new kind of sense.

A few weeks ago, while I was working on this book, my friend Rachel pointed out to me that "Erised" is "Desire" in reverse—just as a mirror flips things from left to right. I felt stupid for not seeing it before. The way this magic mirror works is coded in its name. Likewise, when we hold our longings for romantic love up to the Scriptures, we find they point to a meaning we might not at first have recognized. Our deep desire to be both fully known and unconditionally loved points us to the one true love relationship that none of us can ultimately live without: the neverending love that Jesus has for us.

CLAIM 2:
Jesus Was Silent
on Same-Sex
Relationships

"I think I'm gay."

These words formed in my friend Sam's mind the year he turned 18.[6] Same-sex marriage was not yet legal in the UK, where he lived, and realizing that his sexual and romantic feelings were directed toward other guys was painful and unwelcome news. But that same summer, Sam discovered something even more disruptive. He'd been invited to a church group by some friends and heard the gospel. Like Rachel, Sam soon recognized that Jesus' "offer of forgiveness and deep, wonderful, life-changing love" was just too good to refuse—even though he knew that it would mean not following his heart romantically.[7] So, he said "Yes" to Jesus, and "No" to his same-sex desires.

But was Sam right in thinking that he had to choose between following Jesus and following his feelings? After all, Jesus never explicitly referred to same-sex sexual relationships. Can we conclude from this apparent silence that Jesus is not concerned about the sexes of the people who get married, so long as they live together faithfully? That is the question we'll explore in this chapter.

Jesus' Definition of Marriage

While the Gospels don't record explicit words from Jesus on same-sex sexual relationships, they do record his words defining marriage. One day, some members of a Jewish sect known as the Pharisees asked Jesus, "Is it lawful to divorce one's wife for any cause?" Jesus took them back to Genesis:

> Have you not read that he who created them from the beginning made them male and female, and said, "Therefore a man shall leave his father and his mother and hold fast to his wife, and the two shall become one flesh"? So they are no longer two but one flesh. What therefore God has joined together, let not man separate. (Matthew 19:4-6)

Jesus quotes two verses in his answer: Genesis 1:27, where God makes humans "male and female," and 2:24, where marriage is defined as a one-flesh union between a man and a woman. The second quote alone would be enough to justify Jesus' teaching against divorce. So it's significant that he quotes Genesis 1:27 too. Jesus is emphasizing that marriage unites male and female:

opposite-sex pairings, not same-sex ones. But if it's true that same-sex sexual relationships aren't an option for Jesus' followers—and, as we'll see, other parts of the New Testament say that that's the case—then why didn't Jesus himself explicitly say that?

Jesus' Jewish context

Last summer, I did some speaking in Australia. One of the small but striking differences between Australia and both Britain (where I come from) and the US (where I live) is that most public toilets in Australia have signs warning users not to stand upon the toilet seat and squat. For Western visitors, these signs are bewildering. I wouldn't dream of standing on a toilet seat! But many tourists in Australia are from East Asian countries, where public toilets are designed for squatting. In fact, someone from East Asia might see a Western toilet and think, "Why on earth would someone sit where other people have already sat?"

The reason why certain prohibitions are found in other parts of the New Testament but not in the Gospels is similar to the reason why "Don't squat on the toilet" signs are found in Australia but not in other culturally Western countries: it's to do with the audience. Jesus' ministry was almost exclusively directed to his fellow Jews. As we'll see in chapter 4, the Old Testament explicitly prohibited male-male sex, so Jews of Jesus' day were not debating whether same-sex sexual relationships were allowed. By contrast, the apostle Paul, who wrote many other parts of the New Testament, was sent to spread the gospel to non-Jews (Gentiles) in the Greco-Roman empire. For Greek and Roman men, same-sex sexual relationships were permissible in certain contexts (more on this later). So Paul explicitly addressed this question.

We see a similar differentiation when it comes to idol worship. While Paul addresses idol worship multiple times, Jesus doesn't mention it. This is not because Jesus thinks idolatry is no big deal. It's forbidden in the Ten Commandments, a central passage of the Jewish law. But precisely because of this, the Jews who made up Jesus' audience already knew that idol worship was wrong, so it didn't need to be explicitly addressed. By contrast, many Gentile Christians had once worshiped idols—just as many of them would once have had same-sex sexual relationships—so Paul addresses both these things head on.

This doesn't mean that Jesus was naively unaware of the sexual practices of Greco-Roman culture or that he said nothing that challenged them. In fact, Jesus' teaching on sexual sin cut to the heart of every version of it found in the 1st-century pagan culture around him, and similarly for every version of it found in our society today—including sexual sins that you and I are guilty of, whether we realize it or not.

Jesus' Teaching on Sexual Immorality

People sometimes suggest that Jesus is not concerned with sexual sin. But this could not be further from the truth. In his famous "Sermon on the Mount," Jesus took the seventh of the Ten Commandments (which homes in on sexual sin) and drove it deep into the inner self:

> *You have heard that it was said, "You shall not commit adultery." But I say to you that everyone who looks at a woman with lustful intent has already committed adultery with her in his heart.*
> *(Matthew 5:27-28)*

According to Jesus, all of us are sexual sinners. What's more, the origin of all our sinful thoughts and words and deeds is not primarily our culture, upbringing, or friendship groups but our hearts. "For out of the heart," Jesus explains, "come evil thoughts, murder, adultery, sexual immorality, theft, false witness, slander. These are what defile a person" (15:19-20).[8]

If we look carefully at Jesus' illustrative list of sins, we'll find that same-sex sexual relationships are certainly included. In addition to adultery, Jesus mentions "sexual immorality"—or, in the original Greek of the New Testament, *porneia*. As historian Kyle Harper explains, in Jewish writings around the time of Jesus, "*porneia* could be used to describe a whole array of improper sexual configurations: incest, prostitution ... homosexuality, and unchastity."[9] In the Greco-Roman empire within which the Jews of Jesus' day were living, it was common for men to sleep with other males. Jesus' condemnation of *porneia* would have included that. As an analogy, if I said, "Looking at pornography is wrong," you wouldn't need me to mention gay pornography separately to know it was included in my statement.

People sometimes argue that same-sex sexual relationships can't be wrong because same-sex desire seems to crop up in some humans naturally. In my life, for example, feelings of attraction toward certain women haven't needed to be manufactured. They've come out of my heart. But according to Jesus, the fact that something comes out of my heart or yours does not mean it isn't sinful. The label on our sinful thoughts and actions always reads, "Made in the heart."

But if we listen to Jesus' words, they also guard against the opposite mistake of putting same-sex sexual desire in its own, uniquely sinful category. People who grew up in church experiencing attraction toward members of their own sex can often feel like they're more innately sinful than the person next to them, who might be prone to sinful desire toward members of the opposite sex. But Jesus' diagnosis of the human heart is profoundly levelling. The fact that my heart tends to manufacture same-sex attraction while someone else's typical temptations have a different object does not put me in a special category. When it comes to sexual sin—

as with a hundred other kinds of sin—Jesus looks into your heart and mine and finds us both unquestionably guilty. But, at the same time, Jesus looks into your eyes and mine and tells us that we're unimaginably loved.

Jesus' Love for Sexual Sinners

While Jesus was extremely hard on sin of every kind, he radically welcomed sinners. When the Pharisees complained that Jesus was eating with "tax collectors and sinners" (likely including people known for sexual sin), Jesus replied, "Those who are well have no need of a physician, but those who are sick. I came not to call the righteous, but sinners" (Mark 2:17). The Pharisees just failed to realize they were sinners too. Likewise, when "a woman of the city, who was a sinner," poured out her love on Jesus because he had forgiven her sins, Jesus commended her faith and shut down the self-righteous Pharisee who despised her (Luke 7:36-50). Jesus shocked religious leaders by telling them that prostitutes were getting into the kingdom of heaven ahead of them. Why? Because the prostitutes repented (Matthew 21:28-32). In one of the most memorable stories from the Gospels, Jesus rescued a woman caught in adultery from being stoned (John 8:3-11). And Jesus rescues sexual sinners to this day. Jesus claimed he came "to seek and save the lost" (Luke 19:10). If you feel broken by your sexual sin today, Jesus sees you and says, *You're just the person I was looking for.*

"If it was a choice between following an ancient religious leader or fulfilling my sexuality," my friend Sam observes, "it would be hard not to argue in favor of the latter. But that is not the actual choice I face."

> Jesus is not a religious leader from many centuries ago. I believe him to be my **Creator**: the one who not only made me but came up with the idea of me in the first place. He thought me up! He knows far, far better than I do how I should live. He knows me more than I know myself and loves me more than I love myself.[10]

Jesus wasn't silent when it came to God's design for marriage as male-female. He warns us against all forms of sex outside of that relationship. But if we put our trust in him, we don't need to pretend we are not tempted toward sexual sin, and we don't need to try to hide the times we fail. He knows our thoughts and hearts, and nonetheless he loves us more than any other human—male or female—ever could. Don't set your heart on anyone less wonderful than Jesus.

CLAIM 3:
God's Judgment on Sodom Isn't a Judgment on Same-Sex Relationships

When my friend Paige started out in college, she found herself surrounded by a sex-first, maybe-date-later culture. It was very unappealing, but it seemed like this was just the deal. For any chance of love, she needed to be ok with hooking up. But then Paige noticed her attraction to a female friend and was excited to discover that her feelings were reciprocated. At last, this felt like love.

For some time, Paige and her girlfriend kept the nature of their relationship secret. Paige had been raised in church and felt some anxiousness about disclosing it. But in the end, Paige decided it was time to come out. Her friends were quick to celebrate her sexuality. But her parents were not. In fact, when Paige told them that she was moving in with her girlfriend, they were devastated. Not knowing what else to do, they told her to get her stuff out of her bedroom. As long as Paige was with her girlfriend, she would not be coming home. Paige found this response extremely painful. But she was in love, and that would have to be enough.

Paige didn't like to think that she was walking away from Christianity as she moved in with her girlfriend. So she went to see a pastor from a church that did affirm same-sex relationships to hear a different view. One of the things this pastor told Paige was that Christians have misapplied the story of God's judgment on Sodom. The men of Sodom had attempted gang rape, which was evidently wrong; God's judgement on Sodom was not remotely proof that God opposed monogamous same-sex relationships. In this chapter, we'll explore that claim.

God's Judgment on Sodom

In Genesis 18, Abraham (the founding father of the Jewish nation) was visited by angels with the good news that after decades of infertility, his wife Sarah would soon get pregnant and give birth to a son. But there was also bad news. God was going to destroy the city of Sodom, where Abraham's nephew Lot lived, because of the great sinfulness of its inhabitants. Abraham appealed to God to spare Sodom if he found just 50 righteous people there. God agreed. Abraham asked, *What if there are only 45?* God said he'd spare the city for the sake of the 45. Abraham kept asking until the number of righteous people was down to ten.

Finally, the angels went to Sodom. It's something of a cliffhanger. Would Sodom be destroyed or not?

Angels in the Bible are often confused with humans, so we don't know if Lot recognizes that they're angels when they show up at the city gate. But he immediately invites them to stay in his house. When night falls, Lot's insistence that they stay with him rather than just sleeping in the town square is justified, as all the men of Sodom—young and old—surround Lot's house: "Where are the men who came to you tonight?" they demand. "Bring them out to us, that we may know them" (Genesis 19:5). To "know" someone in this context doesn't mean to get acquainted. The mob is wanting to gang rape Lot's guests. Lot responds, "I beg you, my brothers, do not act so wickedly." Then, to our horror, Lot offers up his two daughters instead (v 7-8). The men of Sodom aren't satisfied with this alternative proposal. Instead, they threaten Lot himself (v 9).

Thankfully, the angels intervene before the mob can act. They strike the men of Sodom blind. Then they warn Lot that God is about to destroy Sodom. So Lot, his wife, and their two daughters escape, leaving behind the daughters' fiancés, who have ignored the warning. When the city is destroyed, Lot's wife looks back—despite the angels' clear instruction not to—so she dies as well. Far from finding ten righteous people in the city, the angels get out with only three. And frankly, as we read on in Genesis, it's a stretch to call them righteous.

This thoroughly traumatic story is often cited as proof that God opposes all same-sex sexual relationships. But is that really a legitimate interpretation?

The Sin of Sodom

Clearly, the attempted gang rape by the men of Sodom is portrayed as wicked. But if they had attempted to rape women (Lot's daughters, for example) that would have been extremely wicked too. The whole situation is a million miles away from Paige's loving, monogamous relationship with her girlfriend.

Interestingly, when Sodom comes up later in the Old Testament, sexual sin tends not to be the focus. In Ezekiel, for instance, the Lord says to Jerusalem:

> *This was the guilt of your sister Sodom: she and her*
> *daughters had pride, excess of food, and prosperous*
> *ease, but did not aid the poor and needy. They*
> *were haughty and did an abomination before me.*
> *(Ezekiel 16:49-50)*

This "abomination" could certainly refer to same-sex sex. As we'll see in chapter 4, this word is used in the Old Testament law when male-male sex is prohibited (Leviticus 18:22). But the same word is used in other passages to refer to other kinds of sin.[11]

In the New Testament letter of Jude, we do see Sodom linked with sexual immorality. Jude references "Sodom and Gomorrah and the surrounding cities, which likewise indulged in sexual immorality and pursued unnatural desire" (Jude 7). The phrase translated "unnatural desire" (*heteras sarkos*) literally means "different flesh," so it's possible he's referencing the fact that the visitors to Sodom were angels, not humans. But multiple Jewish texts from the same period indict the men of Sodom for same-sex sexual sin, so Jude could be highlighting this as well.[12] The story of Sodom also comes up in the apostle Peter's second letter. Peter refers to Lot being "greatly distressed by the sensual conduct [*aselgeia*] of the wicked," using a Greek word which is often used together with *porneia* (2 Peter 2:7).[13] So Peter may well be referring to the attempted sexual assault on Lot's guests. But advocates on all sides of the same-sex marriage question would agree that gang rape is immoral, regardless of the sex of those involved. While this is certainly a negative portrayal of same-sex lust, it's hard to form a clear conclusion from these verses about monogamous same-sex sexual relationships.

Jesus' Warning

Jesus refers to the judgment on Sodom multiple times— not as a warning against same-sex sex but as a warning to those who don't repent and turn to him. For instance, he says to a Jewish city in which he ministered, "If the mighty works done in you had been done in Sodom, it would have remained until this day. But I tell you that it will be more tolerable on the day of judgment for the land of Sodom than for you" (Matthew 11:23-24). Jesus says the same about any town or village that rejects the message brought by his apostles (Matthew 10:15; Luke 10:12). This was offensive to Jesus' first Jewish hearers, and it's offensive to us today. Like the people of Sodom, we're all sinners. Like them, we too will face God's judgment if we don't repent (Luke 17:28-30).

In short, when it comes to God's judgment on Sodom, I think the pastor Paige consulted had a fair point. If this story was the *only* evidence we had to answer the question of whether a Christian can pursue a monogamous same-sex relationship, it would be wildly insufficient. But as we'll see in the rest of this book, it isn't. And the story of Sodom is still relevant to all of us today. According to Jesus, God's judgment on our sin is coming. It is just as serious today as on the day when God rained fire and sulfur down on Sodom. But if we repent and put our trust in Jesus, we can escape because he took that judgment in our place. Today, we don't need to flee from sinful cities. We just need to run to Jesus.

CLAIM 4:

It's Inconsistent to Follow the Old Testament on Same-Sex Sex but Not on Shellfish

In his popular book *God and the Gay Christian*, Matthew Vines recalls a moment in his second year at Harvard when he finally asked himself, "Am I gay?" "The answer was obvious," Vines goes on. "It could have been obvious for years, if I hadn't worked so hard to ignore it."[14] Like me, Vines had been raised in church. Like me, he was serious about his faith. Unlike me, he has since concluded that the Bible *does* allow for same-sex marriage. "Even before coming to terms with my sexual orientation, I had been studying the Bible's references to same-sex behavior," Vines recalls. "Some of what I learned seemed to undermine the traditional interpretation of those passages. For instance, Leviticus prohibits male same-sex relations, but it uses similar language to prohibit the eating of shellfish."[15]

People who affirm gay marriage for believers often suggest that Christians who don't are picking and choosing from the Old Testament law. *The Old Testament forbids both eating shellfish and engaging in gay sex*, the logic goes, *so why are you ok with shrimp and not ok with same-sex sex?* Personally, if, as a student, I'd felt free to pick and choose, I'd happily have given up all shellfish if that would have opened up the possibility of same-sex marriage. But is it true that Christians who say no to same-sex marriage but yes to eating shellfish are just being inconsistent? Let's test that case.

Old Testament Commandments

In Exodus, the Bible's second book, God rescues his people out of slavery in Egypt and brings them to a mountain where he tells them how they are to live with him as their God. God's instructions to his people include the famous Ten Commandments and instructions on how they are to make a tent-like prototype of the temple, where God will meet with his people in a special way. In the next book, Leviticus, God gives further instructions about how his people should live, including laws concerning food and sex.

In Leviticus 18, the Lord tells Moses to command the Israelites not to do the things that people did either in Egypt (where they came from) or in Canaan (where they are going). After a list of laws against a range of sexual relationships, God says:

> *You shall not lie sexually with your neighbor's wife and so make yourself unclean with her. You shall not*

give any of your children to offer them to Molech,
and so profane the name of your God: I am
the LORD. You shall not lie with a male as with a
woman; it is an abomination. (Leviticus 18:20-22)

The command against adultery sounds reasonable to many in our culture today. The command against child sacrifice (a common practice for the worshipers of the pagan god Molech) strikes all of us as absolutely right. But the claim that a man sleeping with another male is an abomination sounds offensive. We would understand if the law was limited to adult men molesting boys. But while this law certainly includes that situation, the Hebrew word for "male" in Leviticus 18:22 is the same word as when God made humans "male and female" in Genesis 1:27. This is a blanket ban on all male-male sex, regardless of age.

When God prescribes the death penalty for breaking these commands, our modern hackles rise still further. We might just understand the death penalty for child sacrifice (Leviticus 20:1-5). But the death penalty for adultery seems harsh (Leviticus 20:10) and the death penalty for men who sleep with other males yet more so:

If a man lies with a male as with a woman, both of
them have committed an abomination; they shall
surely be put to death; their blood is upon them.
(Leviticus 20:13)

This punishment does not elevate male-male sex above all other sins. Most of the sexual sins listed also carry the death penalty, as do many sins of other kinds. While the expression "their blood is upon them" seems especially emphatic, it is not limited to this one form of sin.[16] Nevertheless, it's clear that, according to Old Testament law, same-sex sex is a deathly serious offense.

But, as Matthew Vines points out, Christians don't observe the food laws in Leviticus. So why should we still obey this ancient "No" to same-sex sex? The answer lies in the New Testament.

New Testament Application

"Do not think that I have come to abolish the Law or the Prophets," Jesus declared. "I have not come to abolish them but to fulfill them" (Matthew 5:17). This fulfillment means that there are certain Old Testament laws that Christians are no longer called to follow. For instance, the law prescribed a complex sacrificial system—with priests, a temple, and a host of animal sacrifices. Christians no longer need this because Jesus is the real sacrifice for sins: "the lamb of God, who takes away the sin of the world" (John 1:29). But what about the other Old Testament laws?

Broadly speaking, the commands of the Old Testament can be seen as falling into one of three categories. Some laws are specifically declared to be no longer binding in light of Jesus' coming. This includes the food laws (see Mark 7:18-19; Acts 10:9-16). So Christians can tuck into shellfish without qualms! Other Old Testament laws are not mentioned in the New Testament—or are referenced in ways that leave substantial room for interpretation. For instance, the question of how Christians should observe the Sabbath (the day of rest) would fall into this category. The third category is laws which are explicitly reasserted for Christians. For instance, as we saw in chapter 2, Jesus reasserts the law against adultery. And as we'll see in chapters 5, 7, and 8, the Old Testament prohibition on same-sex sex is reaffirmed multiple times. So saying no to same-sex sex and yes to shellfish isn't picking and choosing. It's following New Testament directives.

While the laws against adultery and same-sex sex still stand, however, every death sentence prescribed in the Old Testament law was taken on by Jesus on the cross. We get a hint of this when a woman caught in adultery is brought to Jesus. To try and catch him out, the Pharisees ask Jesus if she should be stoned to death. Jesus replies, "Let him who is without sin among you be the first to throw a stone at her" (John 8:7). One by one, they walk away. Finally, Jesus is left alone with the woman. "Has no one condemned you?" Jesus asks. "No one, Lord," she replies. "Neither do I condemn you," Jesus responds. "Go, and from now on sin no more" (v 10-11). Jesus is the only person with the right to condemn this woman. But he does not. Rather than setting a model for Christians to continue with the Old Testament legal punishments, Jesus set a model for forgiveness—not because there is no price to pay for sin, or because he doesn't care about how we use our bodies sexually, but because he came to pay the price on our behalf.

Jesus did not turn away from sexual sinners, declaring that "their blood is upon them." Instead, he poured out his own blood for the forgiveness of their sins (Matthew 26:28). Yet, with the same breath that he spoke words of mercy to the woman caught in adultery, he also commanded her not to continue in her sin. Matthew Vines' conclusion—that monogamous same-sex sexual relationships are legitimate for Christians—robs people of the opportunity to turn away from sin and feel the force of Jesus' forgiveness. If we won't recognize our sin, we can't repent. But if we do, we'll find that Jesus' blood is powerful enough to wash us clean.

CLAIM 5:
Paul Condemns Exploitative Same-Sex Relationships, Not Consensual Ones

The day Paige told her parents she was staying with her girlfriend, she decided she might as well do something else they'd hate. So she got a tattoo. It's on her ankle and it reads, "VIII.XXVIII"—or "8:28" in Roman numerals. Growing up in church, Paige had learned verse 28 of chapter 8 of Paul's letter to the Romans: "For we know that in all things God works for the good of those who love him" (Romans 8:28, NIV). Surely, Paige told herself, God was with her as she went all-in on a relationship of love.

Paige didn't realize at the time that one of the clearest New Testament passages condemning same-sex sexual relationships is also in Paul's letter to the Romans. But some have argued that Paul was not condemning *all* same-sex sexual relationships but just the unequal and exploitative ones that were so common in the Greco-Roman empire. In this chapter, we'll assess the evidence for that claim.

What Did Paul Say?

The headline of Paul's letter to the Romans is that *everyone* is sinful and *anyone* can be completely saved by faith in Christ alone. After proclaiming salvation by faith in Romans 1:16-17, Paul makes the case that all of us are sinners who need saving. Paul's words on same-sex sexual relationships form part of this case. As we saw in chapter 1, the Old Testament compares God's relationship with his people to a marriage and likens their idolatry to adultery. In the Old Testament, spiritual adultery often went hand in hand with sexual sin (e.g. Isaiah 57:1-13; Jeremiah 5:7; 7:9-10; Hosea 4). In Romans 1, Paul highlights this connection. He describes how people turn away from God and worship idols. Then he writes, "Therefore God gave them up in the lusts of their hearts to impurity, to the dishonoring of their bodies among themselves, because they exchanged the truth about God for a lie and worshiped and served the creature rather than the Creator" (v 24-25a).

After making this more general point about idolatry and sexual sin, Paul goes on to highlight same-sex sex in particular:

> For this reason God gave them up to dishonor-
> able passions. For their women exchanged natural
> relations for those that are contrary to nature; and

the men likewise gave up natural relations with
women and were consumed with passion for one
another, men committing shameless acts with men
and receiving in themselves the due penalty for their
error. (v 26-27)

It's worth noticing that Paul does not *only* target same-sex sexual relationships, as if they are uniquely sinful. He lists a host of other sins that come with turning away from God, including envy, murder, strife, deceit, and gossip (v 28-31). Then Paul declares, "Though they know God's righteous decree that those who practice such things deserve to die, they not only do them but give approval to those who practice them" (v 32).

These verses sound incredibly offensive to our modern Western ears. But before we unpack what they might mean, it's worth noting something here that would have surprised the average citizen of Rome. As historian Kyle Harper points out, the fact that Paul parallels male-male and female-female sex is "strikingly novel and truly momentous."[17] In the Greco-Roman empire, the primary dividing line in sexual acts was not the sex of the two parties but their roles in sex—active or passive. It was generally assumed that men would have sexual outlets other than their wives, and it was not considered shameful for them to have sex with other males, so long as they took the active role. But Paul says nothing about active or passive roles. Rather, by grouping male-male and female-female sexual relationships together, he is focusing on the same-sex nature of the relationships.

Notably, the Greek words Paul uses to refer to men and women in this passage are not the most common Greek words for men and women, but words which could equally be translated "males" and "females." In the Greek translation of the Old Testament (known as the Septuagint), which was widely used by Jews of Jesus' day, the same Greek words appear in Genesis 1:27, when God makes humans male (*arsēn*) and female (*thēlys*). When Jesus quoted from Genesis 1:27 in his definition of marriage, he used these same Greek words (Matthew 19:4; Mark 10:6). What's more, the same word for "male" also appears in the Septuagint translation of the laws against male-male sex in Leviticus 18:22 and 20:13.

The fact that Paul uses these same words in Romans underlines the connection with both Leviticus and Genesis—and helps us to understand what he means when he says that same-sex sexual relationships are "contrary to nature" (Romans 1:26). In Genesis, God made humans "male and female" and told them to be fruitful and multiply (Genesis 1:27-28). Paul presents same-sex sexual relationships as cutting against God's original design.

But given that Paul was writing in a cultural context in which much male-male sex was unequal and exploitative, is it nonetheless plausible that he meant only to condemn this kind of sex—not equal and consensual relationships between two men or women, like Paige's with her college girlfriend?

What Did Paul Mean?

It is certainly the case that much male-male sex in Greco-Roman culture happened in unequal and exploitative relationships. Men having sex with prostitutes and slaves of either sex was seen as a necessary outlet for male libido.[18] Greek culture also recognized relationships between adult men and freeborn teenage boys—a practice known as pederasty. The ideal age for the boy was between sixteen and eighteen, while the man was often in his twenties.[19] The theory was that the young man acted as a mentor to the youth, and these relationships were often idealized and romanticized. It was considered deeply shameful for an adult man to take the passive role in sex, but it was understood that teenage boys could be pursued and could submit sexually.[20] The Romans were much stricter than the Greeks about freeborn males not being penetrated even in their youth, so for them, these romanticized relationships tended to involve a favorite slave.[21]

With this cultural context in place, then, can we limit what Paul says in Romans 1 to unequal, exploitative same-sex relationships, which we would all agree are clearly wrong? I don't think so.

First, while Greco-Roman culture distinguished between the active and the passive partner in any homosexual relationship, Paul does not. In his thought-provoking book, *Does the Bible Support Same-Sex Marriage?*, Preston Sprinkle points out that if Paul had meant only to target exploitative sexual relationships, he could have used words specific to pederasty: *erastes* for the man—or even *paiderastes* ("lover of boys") or *paidophthoros* ("corruptor of boys")—and *eromenos* for the adolescent boy. But he does not. Nor does he mention slaves or prostitutes.[22] Instead, as we've seen, Paul uses the same Greek word for "males" to describe both parties (Romans 1:27). Nothing Paul says targets inequality in age, status, or sex role. Rather, he is pointing back to the Old Testament's blanket prohibition on all male-male sex and expanding it to explicitly include all female-female sex, which was not typically associated with unequal relationships.

Second, the claim that Paul meant only to prohibit same-sex sex that was not properly consensual is undermined by Paul's description of the same-sex partners being "consumed with passion for one another," underlining the mutuality of their sexual acts. While it was common for men to have sex with boys and to sexually abuse those they enslaved, there is also evidence of consensual sexual relationships between men who were social equals in the period when Paul was writing, and of lesbian relationships between consenting adults.[23]

Strikingly, many scholars who *affirm* same-sex marriage for Christians agree that Paul cannot legitimately be interpreted as only referring to exploitative relationships. For instance, in *The New Testament on Sexuality*, William Loader concludes that Paul's condemnation of same-sex sex in Romans 1:26-27 included, but was not limited to, pederasty, abuse of slaves, and same-sex sex in idolatrous religious contexts.[24] Likewise, in *Homosexuality and the Bible: Two Views*, Dan Via (who advocates for same-sex marriage) states that he and his coauthor, Robert Gagnon, (who argues against it) "are in substantial agreement that the biblical texts that deal specifically with homosexual practice condemn it unconditionally."[25]

So, recognizing the offensiveness of Paul's words in our own culture, how can we understand what Romans 1 might mean for us today?

What Does Romans 1 Mean For Us?

Acknowledging the strength of Paul's words in Romans 1, Matthew Vines concludes:

> *If someone you love follows Christ but is in a same-sex relationship, he or she would appear to have been swept up by Paul and deposited in the dustbin of condemnation. Paul seems to declare them lost ... and deserving of death.*[26]

This sounds heartless and harsh—until we recognize that Paul's argument in Romans is that, by nature, *all of us* are "lost ... and deserving of death." In Romans 2, anyone who doesn't recognize themselves in Paul's catalog of sins gets a slap in the face for judging others when they themselves are sinners too (v 1-5). Paul's point is not that people in same-sex relationships are uniquely facing judgment but that—apart from Jesus—*all of us* will face God's judgment. The good news of the gospel is that there is "no condemnation for those who are in Christ Jesus" (8:1). But Paul is very clear in Romans 6 that this good news is not a free pass to continue in our sin. Being "in Christ Jesus" means submitting to his lordship over all our life, including how we use our body sexually. So followers of Jesus cannot continue in same-sex sexual relationships, even if they've been endorsed by legal marriage ceremonies.

After four years of dating, Paige and her girlfriend got engaged. The seriousness of that commitment prompted Paige to think more deeply about whether she had made the right decision. This was a very painful moment in her life. But she felt sure that something wasn't right, and she ultimately decided to end the relationship. Paige moved to Boston for a fresh start and began attending our church. She assumed she'd have to hide her past to fit in. But she soon discovered that she is not the only person in our congregation with a history of same-sex sexual relationships, and that following

Jesus doesn't mean hiding our sin but repenting of it. Two years ago, Paige got baptized, and as she's grown in faith, she's been a wonderful encouragement to others.

One night, after Bible study at our house, I asked Paige to explain her tattoo to another young woman who is exploring Christianity with us. Paige quoted the verse, "We know that in all things God works for the good of those who love him" (8:28, NIV). Then she explained, "When I got this tattoo, I thought it meant that God would get on board with my agenda. But now I realize it means the opposite."

CLAIM 6:
Paul Was Condemning Excessive Lust, Not Same-Sex Sexual Orientation

Before she came to Christ, Rachel had a string of sexual partners. She lied and stole for fun. She set out to seduce young women who had never had a same-sex sexual relationship and felt smug about her conquests. In short, she fit the stereotype that some people raised in church expect from those who identify as gay.

But many people in same-sex relationships aren't like Rachel was at all. Perhaps you were raised with that stereotype, but as you've met people who do not fit this profile, you've had to rethink your assumptions. In fact, you may have friends in same-sex relationships who are more faithful, loving, and altruistic than some you know in heterosexual relationships. Because of this, you might be wondering if the "No" to same-sex marriage you were raised with was based on stereotypes, not Scripture.

Truth be told, some churches *have* based their teaching more on stereotypes than what the Bible says, so if that was how you were raised, you might need to work through the things that you were taught. But some who advocate for same-sex marriage argue that Paul's teaching was based on 1st-century stereotypes. Just as many pastors in the 20th century regarded promiscuity as an intrinsic feature of a "gay lifestyle"— and could not envisage a loving, monogamous relationship between two people of the same sex—so too, some argue, people in Paul's day could only see same-sex sexual relationships as expressions of excessive lust. The idea was that people who engaged in same-sex sex could have been satisfied with a heterosexual relationship if only they'd had more self-control.

Matthew Vines is one supporter of this view. He argues that in Romans 1:26-27, "Paul wasn't condemning the expression of a same-sex orientation as opposed to the expression of an opposite-sex orientation. He was condemning *excess* as opposed to *moderation*."[27] In this chapter, we'll evaluate the evidence for that interpretation. We'll look first at Vines' claim about sexual orientation and second at his claim about excessive lust.

Ancient Conceptions of Sexual Orientation

One element of Vines' argument is that Paul did not have our contemporary understanding of sexual orientation. Today we can recognize that some people are just born with an exclusive capacity for same-sex desire, but in Paul's world—so the argument goes— same-sex sex was only seen as an optional extra for people who could be satisfied with opposite-sex sex.

However, in her book on early Christian responses to female homoeroticism, historian and gender-studies scholar Bernadette Brooten writes, "Contrary to the view that the idea of sexual orientation did not develop until the 19th century, [various sources] demonstrate the existence in the Roman world of the concept of a lifelong erotic orientation."[28] As one example, Brooten quotes from a text written by a 1st-century Greek astrologer, claiming that if Venus and the moon are in a particular place when a baby girl is born, she "will be a Lesbian, desirous of women," while if a baby boy is born, "he will be desirous of males."[29] Likewise, if Venus and Saturn are aligned in a certain way, the baby boy will turn out "effeminate" and "one of those in whom one does [something] like what one does in women."[30]

The highly influential Greek philosopher Aristotle (384 – 322 BC) also suggests that some men might naturally want to be penetrated by other men. At the end of a list of what he regards as unusual behaviors, including biting one's nails and eating coal, Aristotle mentions "sexual intercourse between males." He goes on to explain, "In some people these result from nature, in others from habit, as, for instance, in those who have suffered wanton assault since their childhood." Aristotle's next comment cuts against the claim that same-sex sex was always seen as an expression of excessive lust. He writes, "If nature is the cause, no one would call these people incontinent [i.e. lacking self-restraint], any more than women would be called incontinent for being mounted rather than mounting."[31] So Aristotle seems to recognize a range of causes for same-sex desire, including nature—or what might today be called "sexual orientation."[32]

Another striking literary source for the idea of something approximating modern ideas about sexual orientation comes from the Greek philosopher Plato's *Symposium*. The setting is an evening get-together in 416 BC, and the book supposedly records conversations between various male friends concerning love. At one point, the comedian Aristophanes tells a story of human origins in which everyone was originally half of a four-legged creature, until the god Zeus bisected them. Some of the four-legged creatures were composed of a man and a woman, some were composed of two men, and some of two women—which explains why some people are drawn to opposite-sex partners and others to partners of their same sex.[33] Of course, this is a fictional account of someone offering a mythological explanation of same-sex attraction. But the story does suggest that some people were seen as being born with an exclusive capacity for same-sex desire.

So, while it is certainly the case that most same-sex sexual relationships we know of from the Greco-Roman world were undertaken in addition to opposite-sex relationships, we can't say that there was no concept of a person who might be exclusively attracted to their same sex. But can we still nevertheless say that same-sex sexual relationships were only seen as expressions of excessive lust, and so that must be what Paul was condemning in Romans 1?

Is Paul Only Condemning Excessive Lust in Romans 1?

In his helpful exploration of this question, Preston Sprinkle agrees that there is ample evidence that Greek and Roman authors often portrayed same-sex sexual relationships as expressions of excessive lust. For instance, we find this claim in another text by Plato: "The pleasure enjoyed by males with males and females with females seems to be beyond nature, and the boldness of those who first engaged in this practice seems to have arisen out of an inability to control pleasure."[34] But there are also plenty of texts that *don't* portray same-sex erotic relationships this way. For instance, historian Kyle Harper summarizes an argument for male-male love found in one of the dialogues of the 1st-century Greco-Roman author Plutarch: "True eros [sexual love] ... has nothing to do with women. Marriage is a domestic arrangement, more about keeping accounts ... than the soul's ascent; bonding between males ... is the true way to nurture virtue."[35]

When it comes to Romans 1, there's no doubt that Paul *does* condemn excessive lust. He is likely targeting various forms of sex outside of marriage when he describes ⟨ giving people up "in the lusts of their hearts to impurity, to the dishonoring of their bodies among themselves" (v 24). But when he dials in on same-sex sex, he starts with female-female relationships, which were not usually seen as the result of excessive lust.[36] What's more, as Sprinkle observes, Paul's argument does not hinge on excessive lust but on nature:

> *"Desire" (epithumia) and "passion" (pathos, orexis) are considered wrong in Romans 1 not because such desires are excessive—Paul never says they are excessive—but because they are satisfied in a sexual relationship that's deemed contrary to God's will.*[37]

Paul's critique is not focused on people adding same-sex sexual relationships on top of marriage (which would fit better with the excessive lust interpretation) but on people rejecting the male-female bond ordained by God and turning to same-sex sex instead.

The "excessive lust" interpretation is unconvincing even to some scholars who advocate for gay marriage. For instance, in *Scripture, Ethics, and the Possibility of Same-Sex Relationships*, author Karen Keen writes, "The biblical authors appear to be concerned not only with exploitation, excessive lust, and patriarchal customs but also with physical complementarity."[38] Likewise, in *Homosexuality and Civilization*, the late Louis Crompton (who identified as gay himself and was a pioneer of queer studies) observes:

> According to [one] interpretation, Paul's words were not directed at "bona fide" homosexuals in committed relationships. But such a reading, however well-intentioned, seems strained and unhistorical. Nowhere does Paul or any other Jewish writer of this period imply the least acceptance of same-sex relations under any circumstance. The idea that homosexuals might be redeemed by mutual devotion would have been wholly foreign to Paul or any other Jew or early Christian.[39]

Just as Paul's consistent condemnation of same-sex sexual relationships includes exploitative relationships but is not limited to them, so his condemnation of same-sex sexual relationships includes excessive lust and promiscuity but can't be limited to them. So where does that leave us today?

Believing what the Bible says does not require us to grasp onto stereotypes about people who pursue same-sex sexual relationships. Paige, for example, was rejecting heterosexual hook-up culture when she started dating her college girlfriend, with whom she lived faithfully for years.

Rather, believing what the Bible says requires us to recognize that we're all sexual sinners. Instead of clinging onto stereotypes, we need to cling to Jesus. Addressing readers who have cheered along self-righteously as he exposed the sinful practices of Gentiles who had turned away from God, Paul tells them that they're just as bad and if they don't repent, they too are storing up wrath for themselves on the day when God's righteous judgment will be revealed (Romans 2:1-5). This is a sobering rebuke for Christian leaders who have gleefully railed against same-sex sexual sinners as if they themselves stood upon the moral high ground. According to the Bible, none of us stand on that ground. It's Jesus who has the right to judge, not us. Instead, even as we speak with clarity about the Bible's teaching on same-sex sexual relationships, we need to take our cues from Paul, who declared, "Christ Jesus came into the world to save sinners, of whom I am the foremost" (1 Timothy 1:15).

CLAIM 7:
The Word "Homosexual" Wasn't Used in Bibles until 1946—It's a Misinterpretation

My friend Brian has loved Jesus since he was a small child. His mother used to call him a young missionary because he was always asking people, "Do you know that Jesus died on the cross for you?" But when Brian hit adolescence, he realized that he was different from most other boys. Because he loved dance and art and wasn't into sport, he was called "gay," "fag," and "queer" before he even knew what these words meant. But the musical *Rent* came out while Brian was in high school, and it woke him up to what he was experiencing. "It scared me," Brian recalled. "I went to the Bible and read 1 Corinthians 6:9-10 and felt condemnation. Somehow, I never got to verse 11."

The passage in Paul's first letter to the Corinthians that caused Brian so much heartache is one of the two passages at the center of a 2022 documentary, *1946: The Mistranslation That Shifted a Culture*, which claims to have "traced the origins of the antigay movement among Christians to a grave mistranslation of the Bible in 1946."[40]

As the makers of the documentary explain, the word "homosexual" wasn't coined in English until 1892 and didn't appear in Bibles until the Revised Standard Version (RSV) translation in 1946. They point out that some earlier translations used terms referring to men sleeping with boys, and argue that the word "homosexual" was used in the RSV to make it seem like the Bible was against gay people when, in fact, most Christians throughout history had recognized that Paul was condemning adult men molesting boys. Since then, some other translations of the Bible have also used the word "homosexual" when translating this passage. For instance, the 1984 New International Version (NIV), which I read growing up, referred to "homosexual offenders."

So is it true that this translation history has led to decades of misinterpretation? In this chapter, we'll investigate that claim by looking at the Greek word (*arsenokoitēs*), which the RSV translated "homosexuals." We'll examine 1 Corinthians 6:9-11, which is one of the two New Testament passages that features this Greek word. We'll focus on the other passage, from Paul's first letter to Timothy, in chapter 8.

Who Will Not Inherit the Kingdom of God?

Just as in Romans, when Paul mentions same-sex sex to the Corinthians, it is listed alongside other kinds of sin and in the context of the gospel. The 2001 English Standard Version (ESV) translation—which I've mostly used throughout this book because it aims to be as literal as possible—translates Paul's words to the Corinthians like this:

> *Do you not know that the unrighteous will*
> *not inherit the kingdom of God? Do not be*
> *deceived: neither the sexually immoral, nor*
> *idolaters, nor adulterers, nor men who practice*
> *homosexuality [oute malakoi oute arsenokoitai],*
> *nor thieves, nor the greedy, nor drunkards, nor*
> *revilers, nor swindlers will inherit the kingdom*
> *of God. And such were some of you. But you were*
> *washed, you were sanctified, you were justified in*
> *the name of the Lord Jesus Christ and by the Spirit*
> *of our God. (1 Corinthians 6:9-11)*

In the Greek, the words translated "nor men who practice homosexuality" are two distinct phrases continuing Paul's "nor (*oute*) … nor (*oute*) …" pattern. The first word, *malakoi*, is the plural of *malakos*, which means "soft" or "yielding to the touch."[41] Jesus uses this word in the Gospels to describe soft clothing.[42] When applied to men, it could have a variety of inferences, from men who took the passive role in male-male sex to men who were too easily seduced by women.[43] So, by itself, *malakoi* could be connected with same-sex sex but didn't have to be. (For instance, the 1946 RSV Bible that is the subject of the documentary translated *malakoi* as "effeminate.") So, what about Paul's next term: the Greek word that the 1946 RSV translated "homosexuals"?

The word *arsenokoitēs* (or *arsenokoitai* in the plural) seems to have been coined by Paul. It combines two Greek words: *arsēn*, which means "male," and *koitē*, which means "bed"—often in sexual contexts. In the Septuagint, both *arsēn* and *koitē* appear in the prohibition on men sleeping with other males (Leviticus 18:22; 20:13). So Paul's word could literally be translated as "male-bedders" and seems to be deliberately referencing Leviticus.

As we saw in chapter 4, *arsēn* means a male of any age. There is no mention of unequal age or status in 1 Corinthians 6:9-11 or in the Leviticus verses from which Paul draws to coin the word *arsenokoitai*. Also, as in Romans 1, Paul does not use any of the terms specific to pederasty. So, contrary to what the documentary suggests, translations that make this word specific to men sleeping with boys are actually misleading. Paul's word certainly includes that scenario, but there is no evidence that it should be limited to it.

Since they're adjacent in Paul's list, it's reasonable to think that *malakoi* and *arsenokoitai* are referring to the passive and active partners in sex; hence the ESV's translation of the two words together as "men who practice homosexuality." If *malakoi* and *arsenokoitai* do describe the passive and active partners, the fact that Paul condemns the behavior of both parties is a further strike against the idea that his prohibition was limited to the abuse of power. In the cultural terms of the Greco-Roman empire, being the passive partner in gay sex was shameful, while being the active partner was generally acceptable. But Paul places both roles outside what is acceptable for those who will inherit the kingdom of God. If Paul meant something else by *malakoi*, however—perhaps men who are easily seduced by women—it's still clear that *arsenokoitai* refers to men who sleep with other males.

So the documentary's claim, that the 1946 RSV imposed an illegitimate meaning on Paul's text and that this has led to people wrongly thinking that Paul is condemning all male-male sex, is unsustainable. All male-male sex is precisely what Paul *is* condemning. But there is one important way in which the 1946 RSV translation "homosexual" *has* led to misinterpretation.

The Real Misunderstanding

The word "homosexual" was coined in 1892 to describe what many today would call a *sexual orientation*: a consistent pattern of attraction toward one's own sex. The word Paul coined, however, anchors not on a pattern of attraction but on action. Paul is not saying that men like Sam or Brian, who find themselves at times attracted to other men, will not inherit the kingdom of God; he is saying that men who sleep with other males will not inherit the kingdom of God. The challenge is that our culture tends to conflate attraction with action, so words like "homosexual" or "gay" are used to describe both someone who experiences same-sex attraction and someone who pursues same-sex sexual relationships. Since modern Western culture assumes that same-sex desire is good, that it must not be questioned or resisted, and that our patterns of attraction are innate to our identity, we struggle to find language for someone who is drawn to their same sex but chooses *not* to pursue their attractions.

Due to this conflation of attraction and action, the translation of *arsenokoitai* as "homosexuals" can cause genuine confusion. It can make Paul's statement about those who pursue same-sex *sex* sound like he is excluding *people* who (like me and Brian) sometimes have to battle with unwanted same-sex attraction. But Brian and I are moral agents, so our actions aren't dictated by our attractions. For comparison, when Paul says in the same verse that adulterers will not inherit the kingdom of God, he's not saying that married people who sometimes have to battle with unwanted attraction toward someone other than their spouse are disqualified from the kingdom. He's saying that married people who follow those attractions and do not repent will be disqualified.

To be clear, this doesn't mean that same-sex attraction is morally neutral, any more than the desire to commit adultery is morally neutral. The Bible diagnoses us as sinners to the core, so even our desires are all messed up by sin. But those who have repented and believed and put their trust in Jesus are assured of God's forgiveness, and we're called to fight against our sinful tendencies, whatever form they take.

Christians who wrestle with same-sex attraction have often been told that if they really trust in Jesus, their same-sex attraction will evaporate—either by a sudden act of God or by ongoing effort on their part. Of course, the God of all the universe is more than capable of doing this, and sometimes he does simply remove temptation. More commonly, Christians might experience a lessening of sexual temptation over time. But the expectation that a truly faithful Christian will not have to battle with same-sex attraction in the long term has left many feeling crushed, alone, or doubting their salvation. Just as many faithful Christians will spend years battling with a desire for adultery (the sinful practice Paul highlights right next to same-sex sex in 1 Corinthians 6:9), so many faithful Christians will spend years battling with same-sex attraction. Followers of Jesus are not promised that they'll never be tempted toward sin. Rather, we are promised that the Holy Spirit of God will help us to resist temptation. What's more, as Paul declares in this same passage, the precious blood of Jesus is enough to pay for all our sin, if we will just repent: "And such were some of you," Paul writes. "But you were washed, you were sanctified, you were justified in the name of the Lord Jesus Christ and by the Spirit of our God" (1 Corinthians 6:11).

Washed, Sanctified, Justified

Tragically, the boys who bullied Brian when he was a kid would have fit right in at many churches of the time. Like so many Christians who grow up experiencing unwanted same-sex attraction, Brian feared rejection by his church and family if he shared what he was going through. He wanted to get married and have kids, so he went off to a Christian college praying that he'd just stop being attracted to other guys and find a girl to marry. But that didn't happen.

Two decades later, Brian's patterns of attraction haven't changed. But so much else has. After years of being scared to share his struggles, he slowly started talking with fellow believers. To his surprise, instead of being met with condemnation or embarrassment, he found that he was met with love. What's more, some years ago, he heard a sermon on 1 Corinthians 6:9-11 that transformed his understanding of the way that Jesus knows and loves him. Brian now sees those verses not as condemnation for those like him who wrestle with same sex attraction but as justification for all who put their trust in Jesus.

Like me, like Sam, like Paige, like Rachel, Brian knows that he's been washed, sanctified, and justified in the name of the Lord Jesus Christ and by the Spirit of our God (1 Corinthians 6:11). The only person who knows us better than we know ourselves—including all our struggles, temptations, and sin—is also the one person who loved us enough to die for us. So now it is our privilege and joy to live for him.

The 1946 translation "homosexuals" is certainly unhelpful to the extent that it obscures this precious truth. But using this moment in translation history to claim that Paul was not writing against same-sex sexual relationships is misleading and unjustifiable.

CLAIM 8:

The Trajectory of the Bible Is toward Rejecting Slavery and Affirming Same-Sex Marriage

As we saw in chapter 6, some advocates for same-sex marriage agree that multiple New Testament verses prohibit same-sex sex. But they argue that this doesn't settle the question, because multiple New Testament verses also affirm slavery. The line of thinking goes like this: *just as we see a trajectory from the Old Testament to the New that moves in the direction of the abolition of slavery, even though it doesn't get there, so we see a progression from the Old Testament to the New that moves toward affirming same-sex marriage, even though it doesn't get there. Christians today can, and should, take that next step.*

This argument is powerful in part because it harnesses the history of slavery in the United States. Between the 16th and the 19th centuries, over ten million enslaved Africans were transported to the Americas, mostly by British traders. Supposedly

Christian countries profited from the systemic abuse of Black people, while many Christian leaders on both sides of the Atlantic tried to justify this using the Bible. In more recent history, many white pastors in the 1960s tried to justify racial segregation using the Bible—while also gladly trumpeting its prohibitions on same-sex sex. It's not surprising, therefore, that many people now see saying no to same-sex marriage as being intertwined with saying yes to slavery and segregation.

So is it true that the trajectory of Scripture is toward rejecting slavery and embracing same-sex marriage? In this chapter, we'll assess that claim. First, we'll look at the Bible's trajectory regarding slavery. Second, we'll chart its trajectory regarding sex and marriage. Third, we'll explore the final New Testament text that explicitly outlaws male-male sex.

The Biblical Trajectory Regarding Slavery

Slavery was endemic in the ancient world, and from the first book of the Bible, we see people being held as slaves. But we also glimpse God's care for the enslaved. In Genesis, God makes promises to Hagar, the Egyptian slave of Abraham's wife, Sarah, who, at Sarah's instigation (and without God's blessing), has become a functional second wife to Abraham. After Sarah throws Hagar out, God tells Hagar to name her son Ishmael, which means "God hears," because he has heard her in her distress. Hagar then becomes the first person in the Bible to give God a name: "a God who sees me" (Genesis 16:9-14, see ESV footnote). This pattern continues in Exodus. Abraham's descendants become enslaved in Egypt. But God sees and hears the enslaved as they cry out (Exodus 3:7). In fact, God's rescue of his people from slavery becomes their founding story.

When God gave the Israelites the law, he frequently reminded them that they were once enslaved (e.g. Exodus 20:2; Deuteronomy 5:6; 15:15). The law banned kidnapping and slave trading: "Whoever steals a man and sells him, and anyone found in possession of him, shall be put to death" (Exodus 21:16). It also included substantial protections for all slaves (v 1-32), while Israelites who sold themselves into slavery were offered freedom in the seventh year and given generous gifts (Deuteronomy 15:12-15). But we need to turn to the New Testament to see the full equality of Jews and non-Jews and the basic assumptions of slavery upended.

In the Roman Empire into which Jesus was born, at least ten percent of residents were slaves.[44] Many were worked to the bone and physically abused. Others were skilled professionals, earning money and living more comfortably than many free people. Some sold themselves into slavery. Others earned enough money to buy their freedom. But one assumption was ubiquitous: slaves existed to serve their masters. It was therefore completely shocking when Jesus told his disciples that his kingdom would reverse that rule: "Whoever would be great among you must be your servant," Jesus explained, "and whoever would be first among you must be slave of all. For even the Son of Man [Jesus] came not to be served but to serve, and to give his life as a ransom for many" (Mark 10:43-45).

Jesus reinforced this radical teaching both in his life and in his death. He taught that he was the master who serves (Luke 12:35-40), and on the night when he was betrayed, he astonished his followers by washing their feet—a task usually reserved for slaves (John 13:1-20). Most stunningly of all, when Jesus was crucified, he died a death that Romans mostly used for slaves. So, in Jesus, we see the rightful King of all the universe embracing a slave's role, dying a slave's death, and calling those who follow him to see themselves as slaves of all.

Following Jesus' lead, Paul called himself a "slave of Christ Jesus" (Romans 1:1; Philippians 1:1)[45] and taught that there was radical equality within the church: "Here there is not Greek and Jew, circumcised and uncircumcised, barbarian, Scythian, slave, free; but Christ is all, and in all" (Colossians 3:11). Paul is often seen as supporting slavery because he called Christian slaves to work hard for their masters. But the reason he gave was not that slaves were inferior (as the paradigm of slavery assumed) but that they were really serving

Jesus (v 22-25). Conversely, Paul commanded masters to treat their slaves "justly and fairly" because they had a "Master in heaven" (4:1).[46] Paul further undermined the master/slave distinction by arguing that Christian slaves were Jesus' freedmen, while Christian free people were Jesus' slaves (1 Corinthians 7:21-23).

We see Paul's ethics worked out in practice when he advocates for a man named Onesimus, who had run away from his master. Under Roman law, Philemon (Onesimus' master) could have punished him severely. But Paul instructs Philemon to welcome Onesimus back, "no longer as a bondservant" but as "a beloved brother" (Philemon v 16). What's more, Paul calls Onesimus his "very heart" (v 12) and tells Philemon to receive Onesimus as he would receive Paul himself (v 17). Here, Paul upends the ancient master/slave hierarchy and recasts it as a brother/brother relationship of love.

So, when it comes to slavery, we do see a trajectory in the Bible from protections and provisions in the Old Testament to the radical reversal of the master-slave relationship that Jesus both commanded and embodied. In light of this, it is not surprising that Christianity was mocked in the 2nd century for being so attractive to slaves.[47] It's also not surprising that the first known wholesale argument against slavery was made by a Christian leader in the 4th century, or that the spread of Christianity triggered the progressive eradication of slavery in Europe, from the 7th century onward. What's completely shocking is that man-stealing and slave trading started up again in Europe in the 16th century, after slavery had been formally condemned as sinful by the church.[48]

While slavery in the ancient world was generally not race-based, those who tried to justify enslavement of Africans from the Bible attempted to portray Black people as innately inferior because of their race. But the Bible stands emphatically *against* racism. Jesus broke through all the racial barriers of his day and commanded his disciples to make disciples of all nations (Matthew 28:18-20). In Acts, we read the first recorded testimony of a Black believer (Acts 8:26-39), and we see a radically multiracial, multiethnic church (2:5-41). The ideas of white supremacy and Black inferiority that were required for the system of race-based slavery are utterly against the Bible, which is oriented around a brown-skinned, Middle-Eastern Savior who welcomes followers from every tribe and tongue and nation.

In summary, you can shoot an arrow from a host of Bible texts to pierce the heart of race-based chattel slavery. The abolition of slavery is not explicitly demanded in the Bible, but the upending of the paradigm of slavery is clear. The abolition of slavery is indeed the natural outworking of New Testament ethics.

So can we say something similar about same-sex marriage, based on a similar trajectory from the Old Testament to the New?

Biblical Trajectories Regarding Sex and Marriage

If we look at the Bible's trajectory when it comes to sex and marriage, we find it's actually toward a more emphatic underscoring of God's original design for marriage as one man and one woman (Genesis 2:24). For instance, while the Old Testament does not endorse polygamy and generally portrays it negatively, it does not outlaw it. But Jesus defines marriage as a one-flesh unity between one man and one woman (Matthew 19:4-6). In line with this, while many leaders in the Old Testament had multiple wives, Paul requires that leaders in the church have (at most) one wife (1 Timothy 3:2). Likewise, Jesus' teaching on divorce and adultery tightens up Old Testament law and reinforces the idea that marriage between one man and one woman is the only place for sex (Matthew 5:27-28; 19:1-6).

When it comes to same-sex sexual relationships, rather than calling into question the Old Testament's "No" to men sleeping with males, the New Testament doubles down on it. While there are two explicit texts condemning same-sex relations in the Old Testament (Leviticus 18:20; 20:13), there are at least three in the New (Romans 1:26-28; 1 Corinthians 6:9-11; 1 Timothy 1:9-11).[49] While the Old Testament specifically outlawed men sleeping with men, Paul also explicitly outlaws women sleeping with women (Romans 1:26).

Those who argue for a trajectory toward affirming same-sex marriage point to the greater evidence for the equality of women in the New Testament compared to the Old, citing Paul's famous declaration:

> There is neither Jew nor Greek, there is neither slave nor free, there is no male and female, for you are all one in Christ Jesus. (Galatians 3:28)

The argument goes something like this: *Just as Paul erases the Jewish distinction between Jew and Gentile and the Roman distinction between slave and free, so he erases the distinction between male and female. If there is "no male and female" in the church, this opens the door to sex difference not mattering in marriage.* The first problem with this argument is that Paul explicitly prohibits same-sex sex. The second is that Paul evidently didn't intend to erase the distinction between male and female since, in his other letters, he calls men and women to different roles.[50] Rather, these verses are intended to describe the unity and equality of Christians, regardless of ethnicity, status, or sex.

What can we make of the fact that instructions to slaves and instructions to wives are given in the same texts? For instance, Matthew Vines points to the "likewise" in 1 Peter 3:1 and claims that "Peter told wives to submit to their husbands *in the same way* slaves were instructed to submit to their masters."[51] But if we look more closely at the text, we'll find that Peter is calling both slaves and wives to model their behavior on that of Jesus himself (2:21-25) and that he uses the exact same Greek word for "likewise" when he gives instructions to husbands (3:7). What's more, a few verses earlier, Peter calls all Christians (male or female, enslaved or free) to live as slaves of God (2:16).

While the New Testament radically undermines the practice of enslaving, it does not do so because *no* human being should serve another human being, but rather because *every* human being should serve Jesus and therefore serve others. But the final blow to what we might call the trajectory argument is that one of the New Testament's clearest strikes against enslavement comes immediately after one of its clear rejections of same-sex sex.

No to Enslaving, No to Same-Sex Sex

In Paul's first letter to his mentee Timothy, he writes:

> *The law is not laid down for the just but for the*
> *lawless and disobedient, for the ungodly and*
> *sinners, for the unholy and profane, for those who*
> *strike their fathers and mothers, for murderers, the*
> *sexually immoral, men who practice homosexual-*
> *ity, enslavers, liars, perjurers, and whatever else is*
> *contrary to sound doctrine. (1 Timothy 1:9-10)*

The word translated "men who practice homosexuality" is *arsenokoitēs*—the same word Paul used in

81

1 Corinthians 6:9. Paul's very next word condemns men who capture people to enslave them. Both these practices are against the Old Testament law. If Paul's condemnation of enslavers here had been obeyed, the transatlantic slave trade would have been impossible. This passage shows that it is perfectly consistent to condemn the history of slavery in America *and* to reject same-sex marriage. In fact, it's what the New Testament demands.

Once again, instead of looking down on sexual sinners from a moral high ground, Paul describes himself a few verses later as the worst sinner he knows, saved only to show that someone as bad as him could receive mercy (1 Timothy 1:15-16). Christians who want to follow Scripture must uphold the Bible's "No" to same-sex sex in any context. But they must do so with humility and with an equally emphatic "No" to racial prejudice and exploitation.

In the Bible's last book, we get a glimpse of the endpoint of all biblical trajectories. We see those who sold human beings as slaves lamenting (Revelation 18:13, 15), and we see sexual immorality outlawed one final time (22:15). We see a countless multitude from every tribe and tongue and nation worshiping Jesus together (7:9-11). We see the church as Jesus' bride (22:17)—the ultimate reality to which Christian marriage points. And we see those who have had their robes washed by Jesus—including repentant sexual sinners of all kinds—enter his city to enjoy eternal life (22:14). This is the endgame.

CLAIM 9:
Unchosen Celibacy
Yields Bad Fruit

"What would you tell your 18-year-old self?"

I was doing a Q&A for teens alongside a pastor in his fifties when this question was asked. The pastor recalled wondering, aged 18, how he was going to keep on following Jesus if his same-sex attraction continued in the long term. The possibility that he might have to fight these desires all his life felt so daunting.

Many today would say that telling an 18-year-old in this situation that there is no path for them to find a same-sex partner is both cruel and dangerous. Matthew Vines tells the story of his friend Stephen, who, as a young man, found himself in the same position as this pastor. "After much study and prayer," Vines writes, "Stephen has developed an affirming view of same-sex relationships. But his non-affirming stance crippled him with depression, anguish, and loneliness for as long as he embraced it."[52]

Vines acknowledges that all of Jesus' followers are
called to deny themselves and take up their cross (Mark
8:34) and that some are specifically called to be single.
But he asks:

> Does that call to self-denial mean gay Christians
> should view mandatory celibacy as part of what it
> means for them to follow Jesus? Or should we view
> that approach as causing unnecessary suffering—
> bad fruit, in other words?[53]

In this chapter, we'll address the claim that not offering
the option of same-sex marriage yields "bad fruit," and
we'll examine what the New Testament teaches about
singleness.

Does Saying No to Same-Sex Marriage Yield Bad Fruit?

Vines draws his "bad fruit" metaphor from Jesus'
warning in Matthew 7:15-18.[54] "Jesus's test is simple,"
Vines writes. "If something bears bad fruit, it cannot
be a good tree."[55] He argues that it was the experience
of the good fruit of Gentile Christians' faith that led
to them being included in the early church without
becoming Jews, and that it was the bad fruit of
suffering produced by enslavement that led Christians
in the 19th century to rethink what the Bible says
on slavery. Likewise, Vines suggests, recognizing the
bad fruit of "unchosen celibacy" for Christians who

experience intense same-sex attraction should lead us to rethink what the Bible says about same-sex sex. But there are multiple problems with this argument.

First, the "bad trees" in Jesus' analogy are false prophets, not false teaching. Second, even if the bad trees did represent false teaching, Vines would need to show that upholding the Bible's clear "No" to same-sex sex *is* false teaching—which, as we've already seen in this book, means riding roughshod over multiple texts. Third, the inclusion of Gentiles is a completely illegitimate analogy. Multiple New Testament texts explicitly affirm Gentile inclusion as a command from God; it didn't just arise because the "good fruit" of Christian Gentiles was recognized aside from Scripture.[56] Fourth, as we saw in chapter 8, multiple Bible texts diagnose the horrors of the transatlantic slave trade and its aftermath as sinful. The suffering of the enslaved certainly motivated Christian abolitionists, but they were cutting *with* the grain of Scripture when they recognized this, not trusting their experience *over* Scripture.

Ultimately, we can only discern good and bad fruit on the basis of what the Bible calls good or bad, and the Bible consistently calls same-sex sexual relationships bad. Vines claims that requiring Christians to fight against same-sex sexual desire causes "unnecessary suffering." But while the New Testament presents resisting sexual immorality as being difficult—calling us to flee from it (1 Corinthians 6:18) and to put it to death (Colossians 3:5)—it does not present it as unnecessary suffering. Rather, it is vital to discipleship.

So, what does the New Testament say about singleness?

The Gift of Singleness

When Jesus defined marriage as a lifelong, one-flesh bond between one man and one woman, his disciples responded, "If such is the case with a man and his wife, it is better not to marry." Jesus replied:

> Not everyone can receive this saying, but only those to whom it is given. For there are eunuchs who have been so from birth, and there are eunuchs who have been made eunuchs by men, and there are eunuchs who have made themselves eunuchs for the sake of the kingdom of heaven. Let the one who is able to receive this receive it. (Matthew 19:11-12)

In the 1st-century Roman Empire, there were many literal eunuchs: men who had been castrated as children so that they could do certain jobs. This is what Jesus means by those who "have been made eunuchs by men." Some people are born with disorders of sexual development (sometimes called intersex conditions) which are discernible from birth. This is likely what Jesus is referring to in his first category: "eunuchs ... from birth."[57] But Jesus' third category seems to be referring to people who remain single "for the sake of the kingdom." There was a strong expectation that Jewish men would marry and raise children. But Jesus radically teaches that there is a unique, missional value to singleness.

This valuing of singleness makes sense in light of Jesus' last words to his disciples. God's first command to humans was "Be fruitful and multiply and fill the earth" (Genesis 1:28). But Jesus' last command to his disciples was "Go therefore and make disciples of all nations" (Matthew 28:19). Wonderful as the call to parenthood is, the call for Christians is not first and foremost to make babies but to make disciples—and single Christians can be extremely fruitful disciple-makers.

Jesus concludes his teaching on singleness by saying, "Let the one who is able to receive this receive it" (19:12). This echoes his comment on marriage moments earlier: "Not everyone can receive this saying, but only those to whom it is given" (v 11). So Jesus offers a positive vision of both marriage and singleness as states which might be given to believers by the Lord.

Following Jesus' lead, Paul taught an incredibly high view of marriage (Ephesians 5:22-33). And yet, as a single man, he wrote:

I wish that all were as I myself am. But each has his own gift from God, one of one kind and one of another. To the unmarried and the widows I say that it is good for them to remain single, as I am. But if they cannot exercise self-control, they should

marry. For it is better to marry than to burn with
passion. (1 Corinthians 7:7-9)

Why does Paul value singleness so highly? He explains:

The unmarried man is anxious about the things of
the Lord, how to please the Lord. But the married
man is anxious about worldly things, how to please
his wife, and his interests are divided. And the
unmarried or betrothed woman is anxious about
the things of the Lord, how to be holy in body and
spirit. But the married woman is anxious about
worldly things, how to please her husband. I say
this for your own benefit, not to lay any restraint
upon you, but to promote good order and to secure
your undivided devotion to the Lord. (v 32-35)

The point of singleness for Christians is not personal freedom to enjoy life without responsibility but whole-hearted devotion to Jesus. Paul is not advocating for commitment phobia or postponing marriage if you don't want to be tied down just yet. He's arguing for single-minded focus on the Lord. But must this kind of singleness be chosen? What about all the Christians who long to be married but have not had the opportunity?

Must Singleness Be Chosen?

Authors like Matthew Vines and Karen Keen argue that singleness should not be forced on Christians who experience same-sex attraction. "Permanently forgoing marriage is a worthy choice for Christians who are gifted with celibacy," Vines writes. "But it must be a choice."[58] Likewise, Keen declares, "Lifelong celibacy is beautiful and meaningful for those who have the grace and call for it. But it can lead to physical and emotional death for those who do not."[59] Vines argues that since Paul seems to offer opposite-sex marriage as an antidote to sexual temptation in 1 Corinthians 7:1-9, the same kind of offer should be extended to Christians who experience same-sex attraction and find living without sex extremely hard. So, if someone finds their struggle with same-sex temptation very difficult, is it better for them to pursue a same-sex marriage? I don't believe so.

First, since marriage is clearly defined both by Jesus and by Paul as male-female, Paul's advice that "it is better to marry than to burn with passion" (v 9) cannot legitimately be applied to same-sex marriage. Same-sex marriage, from a biblical perspective, is a contradiction in terms.

Second, the fact that a Christian might find something extremely hard does not necessarily mean they are not called to it. For example, when Paul was called to be an apostle, Jesus declared, "I will show him how much he must suffer for the sake of my name" (Acts 9:16). So we cannot conclude that those who find singleness hard have not been given that gift. Many Christians will be single for all or for substantial parts of their lives, with varying degrees of difficulty. Lifelong marriage can be very hard as well, but difficulty in marriage is not grounds for divorce.

Third, while Paul is clear that Christians can exercise freedom when it comes to whether they marry or not, this freedom is not without limits. For instance, Paul says that a Christian widow "is free to be married to whom she wishes, only in the Lord" (1 Corinthians 7:39). Even within this limitation, Paul clearly doesn't mean that a widow is free to marry literally any Christian man she wants. Married men and close relatives are also out of bounds, as well as single men who do not want to marry her. So, while Christians have freedom when it comes to marriage, it's a freedom within substantial limits.

Some Christians who experience same-sex attraction may choose to marry. As we'll see in the next chapter, while some people are only ever attracted to their same sex, this is a relatively small proportion of those who experience same-sex attraction. I know both men and women who are happily married to someone of the opposite sex, while still at times battling same-sex desire. But while we must not tell Christians who experience same-sex attraction that they should not marry, we also have no biblical grounds for pushing them to pursue marriage or suggesting that if they just get married, their same-sex sexual temptation will go away. No Christian enters marriage with the promise that they will never again face sexual temptation.

Is Singleness Uniquely Challenging for Christians Who Experience Same-Sex Attraction?

Both Vines and Keen argue that lifelong singleness is harder for Christians who are exclusively attracted to their same sex. Keen suggests that "a profound difference exists between someone who happens to be single but can actively pursue dating and marriage and someone who is forbidden to do either."[60] She continues:

> *Saying no to temptation is not as difficult when no one is available to tempt one's desires; it's a different story to resist the love of one's life. When straight people fall in love, they marry. When gay people fall in love, they must find the herculean strength to say no, not only in the moment of desire, but to every dream of marriage and family.*[61]

There are undoubtedly unique griefs and challenges for single Christians who experience same-sex desire. I do not want to minimize this. Especially in churches where Christians struggling in this way do not feel able to talk with fellow believers and where single people are not valued and included, it is true that loneliness and isolation are all too common. We'll see how utterly unbiblical this is in chapter 10. But I also know single Christians who experience great pain precisely because they feel unwanted by members of the opposite sex. As my friend Dani explains, "There can be a unique sort of grief and pain at having the door to marriage and children always left cracked open while knowing your opportunity and likelihood of being able to walk through that door ever diminishes."

But if the ultimate purpose of marriage is to point us all to the much greater love of Jesus for his people, every long-term single Christian can find hope in knowing that they will one day be included in the only marriage that will matter in the end. In fact, faithful single Christians testify uniquely to the unsurpassable goodness of that final marriage. As my friend Sam puts it, "Singleness is a way of saying that because I've got the reality, I don't need the signpost."[62] Sam and Dani are two of the many single Christians I know whose lives are producing exceedingly good fruit.

The Good Fruit of Faithful Singleness

When I first talked with Brian, whose story I told in chapter 7, he was serving at a Christian summer camp for foster kids. "I may never get married or have kids," Brian told me. "But I still have breath in my lungs and something to offer the church. So how does the Lord want me to live? I can grieve the loss of something I have desired, but I can leverage my life for him." Brian has just started at seminary so that he can better serve the church through teaching.

Like Brian, my friend Lou realized that he was attracted to other guys in adolescence. Lou is also single. He just turned 40, and he serves in almost every ministry at our church. "Of course, part of me wishes the Bible wasn't clear on same-sex marriage," Lou told me. "But Jesus has changed my life, so there's no way I can bail on him!" Lou wears a ring made up of silver fish all swimming one way and a lone, golden fish swimming in the opposite direction. "This represents how I'm trying to live," he says. Lou knows he's swimming against the current of our culture. But that is true of every follower of Jesus in one way or another.

I could tell so many stories of single men and women living fruitful lives and saying no to same-sex sexual desire. Some serve in full-time ministry. Others volunteer. Like me, these friends experience both highs and lows, joys and griefs, progress in faithfulness and discouragement in failure. As Sam observes, it's tempting to compare the downs of singleness with the ups of marriage and vice versa.[63] But we Christians must resist this as we fight together for contentment with the life the Lord has given us for now.

I say "for now" because Jesus taught that there will be no marriage when we're raised to new life (Matthew 22:30). Whether we're single or married today, followers of Jesus are running toward eternity with him and each other—an eternity of love so unimaginably great that any human love that draws our hearts today is like a drop of dew compared to a vast ocean. Our longing for deep human intimacy points toward the satisfaction we will find in Christ when we all meet him face to face. Single believers seeking to live in "undivided devotion to the Lord" (1 Corinthians 7:35) point all of us to this eternal hope. But none of us are called to run alone.

The pastor with whom I did that Q&A for teenagers is single. He still experiences same-sex attraction. He serves the Lord with all his heart and lives embedded in his church family. When asked what he would say to his 18-year-old self, he answered with a smile: "Your life will be so good!"

CLAIM 10:
A God of Love Can't Be against Relationships of Love

"I 've just realized. You guys *have* to love me!"

These words tumbled from the mouth of a young woman who had joined our church a month before. Eighteen months earlier, this new sister in the Lord would have checked all the boxes for the least likely kind of person to become a Christian. Gen Z and raised in a non-Christian home, she had a girlfriend and had etched her sexuality into her skin with multiple tattoos of naked women. But she'd first heard the gospel randomly on YouTube aged 19, and since then the Lord had kept on pulling at her heart. When she was finally ready to repent and put her life in Jesus' hands, she showed up at our church. At our fall retreat, it dawned on her that, unlike any other group that she might join and get rejected from, we have to love her. She is absolutely right.

Signs all across our city make a different claim. The slogan "Love is love" declares that love between two men or women can be just as valuable as love between a man and a woman. For Christians, this can feel persuasive. After all, the Bible states that "God is love" (1 John 4:8). So how can people of the same sex loving one another be against God's will?

The answer is: it isn't.

At this point, you may be surprised to hear me say that. You may be even more surprised to hear I do think Christians have been misinterpreting the Bible on same-sex relationships, and that this misinterpretation has caused substantial harm. In this last chapter, I want to make the case that deep, enduring, sacrificial love between believers of the same sex is not only affirmed but commanded in the Bible—but that it finds its right expression not in the exclusive bond of marriage but in the inclusive bonds of friendship.

Jesus' Commandment

Our culture sees sexual and romantic love as the most potent kind. Its only rival is maternal love. But on the night he was betrayed to his death, Jesus declared to his disciples:

> *This is my commandment, that you love one*
> *another as I have loved you. Greater love has no*
> *one than this, that someone lay down his life for his*
> *friends. (John 15:12-13)*

In the Bible, married love, parental love, and friendship love are all held up as precious. But only this last kind of love is mandatory. As we've already seen, Christian marriage at its best declares that Jesus loves us in an exclusive, flesh-uniting, sacrificial, life-creating way (Ephesians 5:22-33). But Jesus' words on friendship mean that this relationship too must picture Jesus' love for us, as Christians lay down their lives for one another.

Jesus modeled sacrificial love supremely on the cross. But the Gospels also give us glimpses of his love relationships with certain individuals. John calls himself "the disciple Jesus loved" and describes himself leaning against Jesus' chest at the Last Supper (John 13:23-25). Some say this points to a romantic bond. But this just illustrates the shrunkenness of our modern view of nonerotic, nonromantic love. In fact, John's Gospel shows us multiple disciples whom Jesus loved. When Mary and Martha of Bethany send for Jesus because their brother Lazarus is sick, they say, "Lord, he whom you love is ill" (11:3). Not "Lazarus" but "he whom you love." John underlines this love still more: "Jesus loved Martha and her sister and Lazarus" (v 5). We don't see Jesus in the Gospels saying no to love between believers of the same sex. Instead, we see him calling all his followers to love each other just like he loves them.

In modern Western culture and within the church, we've drained the blood from same-sex friendship. Those who want to follow what the Bible says about same-sex relationships must urgently transfuse it back.

Paul's Love Letters

Like Jesus, Paul both models and commands love between believers of the same sex. As we saw in chapter 8, Paul calls Onesimus his "very heart" (Philemon v 12). Likewise, he calls three different Christian men in Rome "my beloved" (Romans 16:5, 8, 9), and Timothy "my beloved child" (2 Timothy 1:2). Paul speaks of how heartbroken he would have been to lose Epaphroditus (Philippians 2:27), and he calls the Christians in Philippi "my brothers, whom I love and long for, my joy and crown ... my beloved" (4:1). The word translated "brothers" here can be used inclusively, so it could also be translated "brothers and sisters," and indeed, Paul had a close relationship with some of the women in the church in Philippi as well (v 2-3). The point is that Paul is unashamed to verbalize his love for fellow Christians, male and female, and he calls believers to express their love for one another physically (Romans 16:16; 1 Corinthians 16:20; 2 Corinthians 13:12).

This is no shriveled view of love between believers of the same sex. It's a robust, expansive, and life-giving love built round our common mission in the world. We are, to use a Pauline image, fellow soldiers (Philippians 2:25; Philemon v 2), "striving side by side for the faith of the gospel" (Philippians 1:27). But this great "Yes" to love between believers comes with an emphatic "No" to any form of sexual immorality. Time and again in Paul's letters, we see commands to brotherly and sisterly love paired up with prohibitions on all sex outside of male-female marriage. Paul writes to the Galatians:

> *Now the works of the flesh are evident: sexual*
> *immorality, impurity, sensuality, idolatry, sorcery,*
> *enmity, strife, jealousy, fits of anger, rivalries,*
> *dissensions, divisions, envy, drunkenness, orgies,*
> *and things like these. I warn you, as I warned*
> *you before, that those who do such things will*
> *not inherit the kingdom of God. But the fruit of*
> *the Spirit is love, joy, peace, patience, kindness,*
> *goodness, faithfulness, gentleness, self control.*
> (Galatians 5:19-23a)

"Sexual immorality" is first on Paul's list of "the works of the flesh." "Love" kicks off the list of "the fruit of the Spirit." Far from producing "bad fruit," the New Testament's strict teaching against sexual immorality is paired with the good fruit of the Spirit.

We see the same contrast between sexual immorality and love in Paul's letter to the Colossians: "Put to death ... sexual immorality," Paul writes, and "put on love" (Colossians 3:5, 14). Likewise, he instructs the Ephesians:

> *Walk in love, as Christ loved us and gave himself up*
> *for us, a fragrant offering and sacrifice to God. But*
> *sexual immorality and all impurity or covetousness*
> *must not even be named among you, as is proper*
> *among saints. (Ephesians 5:2-3)*

The counterpoint to any form of sexual immorality is love. Conversely, any relationship founded on sexual immorality falls short of love. If a friend of mine got legally married to someone of their same sex, however lovingly my friend and his or her partner might act toward each other, it would not make their relationship good because it is founded on affirming sexual sin. If they were not Christians, this would be one of many areas of life that would need to be repented of if they came to believe in Jesus. Likewise, when Christians draw each other into sexual sin of any kind, they're not showing love to one another—however much they might believe they are. Any relationship that's intertwined with sexual sin must be repented of.

We see the opposition between sexual sin and brotherly love with striking clarity in Paul's first letter to the Thessalonians:

> *This is the will of God, your sanctification: that you abstain from sexual immorality; that each of you know how to control his own body in holiness and honor, not in the passion of lust like the Gentiles who do not know God; that no one transgress and wrong his brother in this matter, because the Lord is an avenger in all these things.*
>
> *(1 Thessalonians 4:3-6)*

This stark warning against sexual immorality comes with an equally strong call to sibling love:

Now concerning brotherly love you have no need for anyone to write to you, for you yourselves have been taught by God to love one another, for that indeed is what you are doing to all the brothers throughout Macedonia. But we urge you, brothers, to do this more and more. (v 9-10)

Brotherly and sisterly love is not an optional extra for followers of Jesus. It's a biblical command. We've seen that Paul could not be clearer in his "No" to sexual immorality of all kinds. But he could also not be clearer in his "Yes" to love. In fact, the two go hand in hand.

Is Love Love?

In his first letter, John famously declares that "God is love, and whoever abides in love abides in God, and God abides in him" (1 John 4:16).

I grew up in the Anglican church, and this verse was always quoted in wedding services. But in John's letter, it is not applied to love between a husband and a wife but rather to spiritual siblings in the church. "This commandment we have from him: whoever loves God must also love his brother" (v 21). John makes the point again and again:

By this we know love, that [Jesus] laid down his life for us, and we ought to lay down our lives for the brothers. (3:16)

Beloved, let us love one another, for love is from God, and whoever loves has been born of God and knows God. (4:7)

Beloved, if God so loved us, we ought also to love one another. (4:11)

This isn't sexual or romantic love. But it is vital, powerful, self-sacrificing love designed to imitate Jesus' love for us. Christians must give and receive this love: "By this all people will know that you are my disciples," Jesus declared, "if you have love for one another" (John 13:35). This love is not only to be shown between believers of the same sex. But it is, perhaps, especially to be shown that way. John's focus in his letter is not on male-female love, but on love between brothers (and by extension sisters) in the church. Married or single, we must experience and give this love.

A few months back, my friend Andrew preached on a passage in Paul's letter to the Philippians, where Paul shares his longing to be with Jesus. Andrew illustrated this desire by sharing how he longs to see his best friend, Antony. I know no husband who loves his wife more than Andrew loves Rachel. But his desire to be with Antony—to talk, laugh, work, play, hug, and eat together—is also powerful. I feel the pull of this same kind of love toward my closest friends. But just as my love for my three children pulls on different parts of me than my love for my husband, so my love for my friends is rightfully a different kind of love.

Made for Love

After reading that last sentence, you might be thinking, "Wait! I thought you said you were attracted to women! How come you're married to a man?" I'm often asked how this can be. Did I stop being attracted to women? Is my marriage a fake? Am I saying that everyone who struggles with same-sex attraction should find an opposite-sex spouse ASAP? The answers to these questions are "No," "No," and "No." I've been married to Bryan for sixteen years. I'm deeply thankful for the love we share and for his willingness to marry me fully knowing that I struggled with attraction toward certain women. He took the view that everyone will likely find themselves at times attracted to someone other than their spouse, and whether that attraction is to men or women is beside the point. Over the years, like most married people, there are times when I *have* found myself attracted to someone outside my marriage. For me, that's always been to other women.

You might be thinking that I'm a strange outlier: a woman who experiences significant same-sex attraction, but not exclusively so to the point where she could not be happily married to a man. But actually, I'm very typical. Psychology professor Lisa Diamond (who is herself a lesbian activist) has conducted extensive research and found that about 14% of women experience significant same-sex attraction, but only 1% are exclusively attracted to other women. For men, about 7% experience same-sex attraction, while only 2% are only ever attracted to other men.[64] So women like me, who are attracted to other women but not exclusively, are by far the largest category of people who experience same-sex attraction. For me and for several other women I know, the fact that I don't find other men to be desirable has not prevented me from forming a unique bond with one particular man. But this does not mean that any woman who experiences same-sex attraction could do the same.

Diamond has also found that people's patterns of attraction can change over time. Some people find same-sex attraction cropping up later in life. Others who may have previously identified as gay find themselves in an opposite-sex relationship.[65] This does not mean that no one is exclusively attracted to their same sex all their life. Some people are. Nor does it mean that Christians can simply change their patterns of attraction with enough prayer or effort. As we saw in chapter 7, God is more than capable of removing someone's same-sex attraction, and this certainly can happen—just as God sometimes graciously removes temptation in another area. But followers of Jesus are not promised that they'll never face temptation. Rather, we are promised that the Lord will help us stand and fight against temptation when it comes.

Just as every married Christian must say no to their attractions when they pull them away from their spouse, so must I. I'm profoundly thankful for my marriage. But at times, a piece of me still longs for an exclusive and romantic relationship with another woman—a longing that even the best husband can't fulfill. What I've learned over the years is that my best defense against temptation is to cry out to the Lord for help, repent of any sinful thoughts, press into multiple deep friendships with sisters who know my struggles and temptations and can help me stand firm, and press on with the work that God has put in front of me.

Each week, I have the blessing of connecting with dear Christian friends I love. I get to hug them, laugh with them, talk with them, pray with them, work alongside them, and confess my sins to them. I hear them say, "I love you," and I believe that it is true. As I dig into deep friendship with my sisters in the Lord, I'm following the Scriptures and enjoying the God-given, sisterly love of which same-sex romantic love would be a twisted copy.

You see, the first lie Satan ever told God's people was that God did not really love them. In Genesis 3, the serpent convinces Eve that God's commandment not to eat the fruit of the tree of the knowledge of good and evil is God depriving her of something wonderful. The fruit looked good to Eve. So she decided to believe that God was holding out on her. But, as Paul points out, the God who gave his only Son to die for us is only ever acting for our good (Romans 8:32). The whisper in my ear that sometimes tells me I am missing out by saying no to same-sex sexual and romantic love is a seductive lie. The good things God has given me in marriage and in sisterly love are ultimately better because they're plumbed into the love of Jesus. And the sense I sometimes have of yearning for a greater love than anything I currently experience is pointing me to that great future day when I will meet with Jesus face to face.

Before Dumbledore tells Harry how the mirror works, he gives this hint: "The happiest man on earth would be able to use the Mirror of Erised like a normal mirror, that is, he would look into it and see himself exactly as he is."[66] But the mirror can do nothing to make the watcher's dreams come true. "Men have wasted away before it, entranced by what they have seen, or been driven mad, not knowing if what it shows is real or even possible," Dumbledore warns. By contrast, when we set our eyes on Jesus, we will ultimately get our heart's desire: "Beloved," John declares, "we are God's children now, and what we will be has not yet appeared; but we know that when [Jesus] appears, we shall be like him, because we shall see him as he is" (1 John 3:2). Jesus alone is the perfect image of God; when we gaze on him, we will become like him, and all our dreams of everlasting love will finally come true.

So does the Bible affirm same-sex relationships? A thousand times "Yes!" But for the followers of Jesus, love between believers of the same sex takes a different form from sexual and romantic love. Like married love, it flows from Jesus' self-sacrificing love for us. But unlike married love, it finds its right expression not in one exclusive bond but in a range of love relationships with brothers and sisters in the Lord.

My newly-minted sister could not have been more right when she declared excitedly, "You guys have to love me!" But the converse is true too: she must love us. Two years ago, she was emphatically proclaiming, "Love is love!" Now this precious new believer is declaring with her new-found siblings in the Lord: "By this we know love, that [Jesus] laid down his life for us, and we ought to lay down our lives for the brothers" (1 John 3:16).

Epilogue

I n this short book, I've told multiple stories about Christians who, like me, experience same-sex attraction. Some, like Sam, Brian, and Lou are single. Others, like me, Rachel, and Paige are married. In my home church, I know of seven siblings in the Lord who have a history of same-sex attraction. Since it is a medium-sized church, there are very likely more.

If you're part of a church with a hundred people, it's likely that around ten of them experience same-sex attraction. Some will be single. Others will be married. Some will feel comfortable sharing their experiences. Others will not even have told their closest friends. This means that we should never assume that no one in our Bible study, youth group, church, or family experiences same-sex attraction. Your brothers and your sisters may be wrestling with temptation and feeling alone. They may well need your love and help and prayers. If someone opens up to you, please reassure them that you're with them, like a fellow soldier, ready to support them in the battle.

In her outstanding book, *Born Again This Way: Coming Out, Coming to Faith, and What Comes Next*, Rachel recalls how her friend Sylvia helped her in her early Christian life. When Rachel fell into a sexual relationship with another girl, Sylvia helped her to end it. When Rachel called Sylvia to confess through tears that she had slept with her ex-girlfriend during what was meant to be a "just friends" visit, Sylvia kept telling her to "just come home." She grieved with Rachel over her sin, reassured her of God's forgiveness, and helped her to make the battle plan she needed to flee sexual sin in the future.[67]

Whatever our temptations—and whether our sexual sin is as dramatic as Rachel's was in her first year as a Christian or whether it's a battle in the mind—all of us need friends like Sylvia. And all of us could be a Sylvia to someone else. Sylvia did not seek to love Rachel by affirming her sinful desires or questioning if same-sex sexual relationships are really forbidden by God's word. That was the last thing Rachel needed. Instead, Sylvia loved her sister in the Lord by helping her to repent and pointing her to Jesus.

In 2023, I interviewed Rachel for a podcast episode on what someone who becomes a Christian while legally married to someone of their same sex should do next. At the end of the interview, Rachel quoted one of Jesus' parables:

> *The kingdom of heaven is like treasure hidden in a field, which a man found and covered up. Then*

*in his joy he goes and sells all that he has and buys
that field. (Matthew 13:44)*

Following Jesus means being willing to give up everything—even our most treasured hopes, dreams, and relationships. We tend to see this as a terrible cost. But Rachel pointed out that the man in Jesus' parable does not sell all he has resentfully, lamenting all the way. Rather, he's filled with joy. Rachel movingly reflected, "When you've actually heard the gospel, when you've actually seen the beauty of Christ, you sell everything *in your joy.*"[68] You see, Jesus is the treasure. When we find him, we find our life (Colossians 3:4). And as we give ourselves to Jesus, we will find that we have gained each other too.

The Christian call is not to loneliness but to love. We're meant to need each other. We must listen to each other, help each other, challenge each other, embrace each another, and point each other to the day when Jesus will come back to claim us all together as his bride.

And surely, he is coming soon. "Amen. Come, Lord Jesus!" (Revelation 22:20).

Endnotes

1 Originally published in 1952, a recent edition of the book is: C.S. Lewis, *Mere Christianity* (Harper San Francisco, 2001).

2 You can read more of Rachel's story in Rachel Gilson, *Born Again This Way: Coming Out, Coming to Faith, and What Comes Next* (The Good Book Company, 2020).

3 J.K. Rowling, *Harry Potter and the Philosopher's Stone* (Bloomsbury, 1997), p 153.

4 J.K. Rowling, *Harry Potter and the Philosopher's Stone*, p 157.

5 See also Matthew 9:14-15 and Luke 5:33-35.

6 Sam Allberry, *Is God Anti-Gay?* (updated and expanded edition, The Good Book Company, 2023), p 14. Sam does not refer to himself as "gay" now, as that term carries implications in most people's minds that he does not want to communicate. For a helpful explanation of his thinking here, see *Is God Anti-Gay?*, p 16-17.

7 Sam Allberry, *Is God Anti-Gay?*, p 16.

8 See also Mark 7:21-23.

9 See Kyle Harper, *From Shame to Sin: The Christian*

Transformation of Sexual Morality in Late Antiquity (Harvard University Press, 2013), p 89.

10 Sam Allberry, *Is God Anti-Gay?*, p 33.

11 See, for example, Proverbs 6:16: "There are six things that the LORD hates, seven that are an abomination to him: haughty eyes, a lying tongue, and hands that shed innocent blood, a heart that devises wicked plans, feet that make haste to run to evil, a false witness who breathes out lies, and one who sows discord among brothers."

12 For a survey of these texts, see Tom Schreiner, *1 & 2 Peter and Jude,* Christian Standard Commentary, 2nd edition (Holman, 2020), p 544.

13 See, for example, Romans 13:13; 2 Corinthians 12:21; and Galatians 5:19.

14 Matthew Vines, *God and the Gay Christian: The Biblical Case in Support of Same-Sex Relationships* (Convergent Books, 2014), p 5.

15 Matthew Vines, *God and the Gay Christian*, p 11.

16 The death penalty for a man cursing his father or his mother comes with the same declaration (Leviticus 20:9).

17 Kyle Harper, *From Shame to Sin: The Christian Transformation of Sexual Morality in Late Antiquity* (Harvard University Press, 2016), p 12.

18 See Kyle Harper, *From Shame to Sin*, p 27.

19 See Kyle Harper, *From Shame to Sin*, p 25.

20 Harper quotes from the Greek philosopher Plutarch's *Erotikos* as voicing mainstream opinion: "We place men who take pleasure from the passive role in the category

of the most wicked and allot them no faith, no honor, no friendship." See *From Shame to Sin*, p 27.

21 Kyle Harper, *From Shame to Sin*, p 25.

22 See Preston Sprinkle, *Does the Bible Support Same-Sex Marriage? 21 Conversations from a Historically Christian View* (David C. Cook, 2023), p 89-90.

23 For a summary of this evidence, see Preston Sprinkle, *Does the Bible Support Same-Sex Marriage?*, p 90-97.

24 William Loader, *The New Testament on Sexuality* (Eerdmans, 2012), p 325.

25 Dan O. Via and Robert A.J. Gagnon, *Homosexuality and the Bible: Two Views* (Fortress Press, 2003), p 93.

26 Matthew Vines, *God and the Gay Christian*, p 99.

27 Matthew Vines, *God and the Gay Christian*, p 105.

28 Bernadette Brooten, *Love Between Women: Early Christian Responses to Female Homoeroticism* (University of Chicago Press, 1996), p 140.

29 *Carmen Astrologicum* 2.7.6. See Brooten, *Love between Women*, p 120. Quoted by Preston Sprinkle, *Does the Bible Support Same-Sex Marriage?*, p 113.

30 *Carmen Astrologicum* 2.7.9. Quoted in Brooten, *Love between Women*, p 120. Chapter 4 of Brooten's book examines a range of ancient astrological texts that make these kinds of predictions.

31 Aristotle, *Nicomachean Ethics*, 1148b. Quoted from *Aristotle: Nicomachean Ethics,* trans. Terence Irwin (Hackett Publishing, 1999), p 106-107.

32 My point here is not to comment on the helpfulness or

otherwise of the terminology of sexual orientation, but rather to question the claim that people in Paul's time were simply unaware that someone could be drawn to their same sex in an ongoing and even exclusive way.

33 Plato, *Symposium*, 189-193. See Louis Crompton, *Homosexuality and Civilization* (Harvard University Press, 2003), p 58.

34 Plato, *Laws*, 636. Cited by Preston Sprinkle, "Paul and Homosexual Behavior: A Critical Evaluation of the Excessive Lust Interpretation of Romans 1:26-27," *Bulletin for Biblical Research 25.4* (2015), p 497–517. See also Preston Sprinkle, *Does the Bible Support Same-Sex Marriage?*, p 102.

35 Plutarch, *Dialogue of Love*, 4. Cited by Preston Sprinkle, *Does the Bible Support Same-Sex Marriage?*, p 103.

36 Preston Sprinkle, *Does the Bible Support Same Sex Marriage?*, p 104.

37 Preston Sprinkle, *Does the Bible Support Same-Sex Marriage?*, p 106.

38 Karen R. Keen, *Scripture, Ethics, and the Possibility of Same-Sex Relationships* (Eerdmans, 2018), p 20.

39 Louis Crompton, *Homosexuality and Civilization* (Harvard University Press, 2003), p 114.

40 https://www.1946themovie.com. The argument of the documentary is summarized in this interview with Ed Oxford, one of it researchers: https://www.forgeonline.org/blog/2019/3/8/what-about-romans-124-27.

41 See the entry for *malakos* in *The Complete Word Study*

Dictionary: New Testament (AMG Publishers, 1992).

42 Jesus asks the crowds who followed John the Baptist, "What then did you go out to see? A man dressed in soft clothing? Behold, those who wear soft clothing are in kings' houses" (Matthew 11:8; Luke 7:25).

43 Matthew Vines recognizes both these uses of the term. See *God and the Gay Christian*, p 119-122.

44 Kyle Harper, *From Shame to Sin*, p 45, 26.

45 The Greek word *"doulos"* is translated by the ESV as "servant" in these verses. However, it is the same word used in Colossians 3:11, where it is translated "slave."

46 See also Ephesians 6:5-9.

47 The 2nd-century Greek philosopher Celsus quipped that Christians "want and are able to convince only the foolish, dishonorable, and stupid, only slaves, women, and little children." Origen, *Contra Celsum*, 3.44. Quoted by Michael J. Kruger, *Christianity at the Crossroads: How the Second Century Shaped the Future of the Church* (IVP Academic, 2018), p 34-35.

48 For more on this, see Rebecca McLaughlin, *Confronting Christianity: 12 Hard Questions for the World's Largest Religion* (Crossway, 2019), p 183-187.

49 Some would include Jude v 7 and 2 Peter 2:6-10, which we touched on in chapter 3, in this list as well, since they reference God's judgement on Sodom.

50 See, for example, Ephesians 5:22-33; 1 Corinthians 11:1-16; 1 Timothy 2:8-15.

51 Matthew Vines, *God and the Gay Christian*, p 143.

52 Matthew Vines, *God and the Gay Christian*, p 30.

53 Matthew Vines, *God and the Gay Christian*, p 17.

54 Matthew Vines, *God and the Gay Christian*, p 14. See also Matthew 12:33-35 and Luke 6:43-45, where Jesus uses the same metaphor to make similar points.

55 Matthew Vines, *God and the Gay Christian*, p 15.

56 See, for example, Acts 10; 15; Romans 9:22-33; Ephesians 3:1-6.

57 Many disorders of sexual development are not discernible from birth and may only be identified later in life, as someone goes through puberty or when they start trying to have children. But in the 1st century and today, some conditions are evident from infancy and would have kept people in the 1st century from being able to marry.

58 Matthew Vines, *God and the Gay Christian*, p 44.

59 Karen R. Keen, *Scripture, Ethics, and the Possibility of Same-Sex Relationships*, p 71.

60 Karen R. Keen, *Scripture, Ethics, and the Possibility of Same-Sex Relationships*, p 73.

61 Karen R. Keen, *Scripture, Ethics, and the Possibility of Same-Sex Relationships*, p 73.

62 Sam Allberry, "How Both Singleness and Marriage Testify to the Gospel," *Crossway Articles* (March 10, 2019), https://www.crossway.org/articles/how-both-singleness-and-marriage-testify-to-the-gospel/.

63 Sam Allberry, 7 *Myths About Singleness* (Crossway, 2019), p 31.

64 Diamond summarized her research in a lecture

at Cornell University: "Just How Different Are Female and Male Sexual Orientation?" (YouTube, October 17, 2013), https://www.youtube.com/watch?v=m2rTHDOuUBw. For a short summary on the different proportions of the population that report same-sex attraction, same-sex sexual behavior, and LGBT identity, see Gary J. Gates, "How Many People are Lesbian, Gay, Bisexual, and Transgender?," UCLA School of Law, Williams Institute, April 2011, https://williamsinstitute.law.ucla.edu/publications/how-many-people-lgbt.

65 As Diamond puts it, "Changes in patterns of same-sex and other-sex attraction is a relatively common experience among sexual minorities." Lisa M. Diamond, "Sexual Fluidity in Male and Females," *Current Sexual Health Reports 8* (November 4, 2016), p 249-256, https://doi.org/10.1007/s11930-016-0092-z.

66 J.K. Rowling, *Harry Potter and the Philosopher's Stone*, p 156.

67 Rachel Gilson, *Born Again This Way: Coming Out, Coming to Faith, and What Comes Next* (The Good Book Company, 2019), p 67.

68 Quoted from "Should someone in a same-sex marriage who becomes a Christian get divorced?" with Rachel Gilson and J.D. Greear (The Confronting Christianity Podcast, May 23, 2023).

Read More on This Subject

Over 200,000 copies sold. Updated and Expanded

IS GOD
ANTI-GAY?

And Other Questions About Jesus,
the Bible, and Same-Sex Sexuality

SAM ALLBERRY

Foreword by TIMOTHY KELLER

A sensitive exploration of Jesus' teaching on
sexuality, showing how the gospel is good news
for everyone, whatever their sexual orientation.

Why does God care who I sleep with?

SAM ALLBERRY

Explores God's design for the expression of human sexuality—what it says about him and what that means for us. Ideal for giving away to people who may see this as a stumbling block for belief.

thegoodbook
COMPANY

thegoodbook.com | thegoodbook.co.uk
thegoodbook.com.au

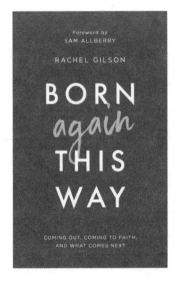

In this powerful and personal book, author Rachel Gilson describes her own unexpected journey to show how it is possible for Christians who experience same-sex attraction to live both faithful and fulfilling lives.

thegoodbook.com | thegoodbook.co.uk
thegoodbook.com.au

thegoodbook
COMPANY

Thanks for reading this book. We hope you enjoyed it, and found it helpful.

Most people want to find answers to the big questions of life: Who are we? Why are we here? How should we live? But for many valid reasons we are often unable to find the time or the right space to think positively and carefully about them.

Perhaps you have questions that you need an answer for. Perhaps you have met Christians who have seemed unsympathetic or incomprehensible. Or maybe you are someone who has grown up believing, but need help to make things a little clearer.

At The Good Book Company, we're passionate about producing materials that help people of all ages and stages understand the heart of the Christian message, which is found in the pages of the Bible.

Whoever you are, and wherever you are at when it comes to these big questions, we hope we can help. As a publisher we want to help you look at the good book that is the Bible because we're convinced that as we meet the person who stands at its heart—Jesus Christ—we find the clearest answers to our biggest questions.

Visit our website to discover the range of books, videos and other resources we produce, or visit our partner site www.christianityexplored.org for a clear explanation of who Jesus is and why he came.

Thanks again for reading,

Your friends at The Good Book Company

thegoodbook.com | thegoodbook.co.uk
thegoodbook.com.au | thegoodbook.co.nz | thegoodbook.co.in

·**WWW.CHRISTIANITYEXPLORED.ORG**

Our partner site is a great place to explore the Christian faith, with powerful testimonies and answers to difficult questions.